# LIGHTHOUSES
## *of* NORTH
## AMERICA

### Beacons from Coast to Coast

# A Firefly Book

Published by Firefly Books Ltd. 2013

First printing

**Publisher Cataloging-in-Publication Data (U.S.)**

A CIP record for this title is available from the Library of Congress

**Library and Archives Canada Cataloguing in Publication**

Jackson, Sylke, author
    Lighthouses of North America : beacons from coast to coast / Sylke Jackson. Includes bibliographical references and index.
ISBN 978-1-77085-249-5 (bound)
    1. Lighthouses—Canada. 2. Lighthouses— Canada— Pictorial works. 3. Lighthouses—United States. 4. Lighthouses—United States—Pictorial works. 5. Lighthouses— Canada—Design and construction— History. 6. Lighthouses— United States—Design and construction—History. I. Title.
VK1026.J33 2013       387.1'550971       C2013-902456-5

Published in the United States by
Firefly Books (U.S.) Inc.
P.O. Box 1338, Ellicott Station
Buffalo, New York 14205

Published in Canada by
Firefly Books Ltd.
50 Staples Avenue, Unit 1
Richmond Hill, Ontario L4B 0A7

Cover design: Erin R. Holmes/Soplari Design

Printed in China

Conceived, designed, and produced by
Moseley Road Inc.
123 Main Street
Irvington, NY 10533
www.moseleyroad.com

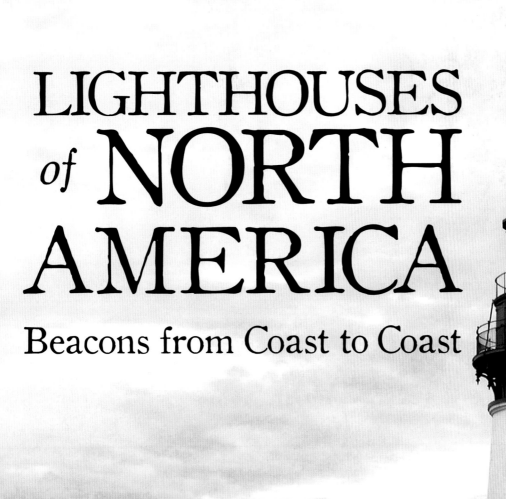

# LIGHTHOUSES
## *of* NORTH
## AMERICA

### Beacons from Coast to Coast

Sylke Jackson

# Contents

◄ **North Head Lighthouse**, Washington

◄ **Cape Neddick Lighthouse**, Maine

# A BRIEF HISTORY OF *Lighthouses*

**The history of lighthouses** is intimately linked to the development of maritime expertise. As great nations advanced their abilities to navigate nearby oceans and ventured into unknown territories, they spent considerable resources on marking significant ports. The first lighthouses were intended to welcome ships and stimulate trade and not until much later were beacons used to warn of dangerous conditions, such as rocky ledges or submerged shoals. The building of lighthouses implies the development of nautical powers. Seafarers were no longer merely at the whim of the elements; they moved to secure their environment to assure the fleet's safe passage. Lighthouses are also a mark of economic stability and efficient centralized government; feudal societies such as the Vikings were home to preeminent sailors but never consolidated funds or organized to build mutually beneficial aids to navigation. The golden age of lighthouses came in the 19th and 20th centuries, when lights proved a strategic asset to a world community that had recently mastered circumnavigating the globe.

*"Far in the bosom of the deep*
*O'er these wild shelves my watch I keep*
*A ruddy gem of changeful light*
*Bound on the dusky brow of Night*
*The Seaman bids my lustre hail*
*And scorns to strike his tim'rous sail."*

— Sir Walter Scott
Written in the visitor's album during his
1814 inspection of the Bell Rock Lighthouse

**The Bell Rock Light** located in the North Sea is the world's oldest surviving sea-washed lighthouse. The light has taken the brunt of heavy waves and winds and survived a helicopter crash in 1955.

Many examples, however, predate this golden age. One of the most famous lighthouses of all time was built on the eastern point of Pharos Island to light the way to Alexandria, Egypt, in the third century BC. The structure, made up of three distinct levels, is estimated to have been almost 500 feet (152 m) tall, with a light visible from 35 miles (56 km) away. Commissioned by Alexander the Great's general, Ptolemy I Soter, designed by Sostratos, and built by thousands of Egyptian slaves, this edifice defined lighthouse technology for more than a millennium. Many languages — including French, Italian, Spanish, Portuguese and Romanian — still use

▲ **The Dover Castle Lighthouse,** built in the first century AD, was originally 80 feet (24 m) tall and octagonal. Only the bottom four floors of the light remain today.

▼ **The Pharos Lighthouse of** Alexandria took 12 years to build and was constructed of marble blocks with lead mortar.

some version of the word *pharos* to mean lighthouse. One of the Seven Wonders of the World in the Hellenistic period, the lighthouse stood until damaged beyond repair by the earthquakes of 1303 and 1323.

Pharos Lighthouse outshone any light that would follow for the next 1000 years after its erection. Some Roman lights, however few, did cast a faint glow over the waters during this period. Built around the first century, the remnants of one of the twin lighthouses at Dover still stand. Its contemporary, the Tower of Hercules, in Spain at A Coruña, functions as the oldest active Roman lighthouse. Recorded information about lighthouses in the next seven centuries is next to nonexistent. The fall of the Roman Empire resulted in decreased trade and a diminished need for navigational beacons. In the ninth century AD, the Chinese hung lanterns at the top of tiered constructions, such as Mahota Pagoda, which still stands in Shanghai. The lit pagoda provided an aid to ships in the Huangpu River and the harbor, which served as an outlet to the Yangtze. Pagodas served primarily as religious temples with only secondary navigational functions. The religious kept lighthouses in Europe as well, and as late as the 12th century AD, monks tended a beacon in Ireland at Hook Head. This lighthouse continues to operate today. Although some lights shone during the Middle Ages, no nautical technological advancements were made; sailors crossing the Mediterranean in 1000 AD took the same amount of time as those in 300 AD.

The lateen sail heralded the next substantial development in maritime history. Used since the third century in the Mediterranean Sea, the lateen was adopted by northern Europeans in the late Middle Ages, and boat builders added these triangular sails to vessels that had previously only included the traditional square-shaped sails. Similar in form to the rig of today's Sunfish sailboat, the lateen sail increased maneuverability and allowed many ships to sail out of the Mediterranean Sea into the Atlantic.

▶▶**Hook Head Light in Ireland was built** in the 12th century. It remained an active aid to navigation throughout its history except for a period of 16 years in the 17th century when civil war broke out. The modern facade encases the centuries-old structure.

▼**The Mediterranean could be treacherous** to travel, and though the construction of lights helped ease the journey, it did not speed it up. It is believed the Romans built at least 30 lighthouses on the Mediterranean.

Armed with this advancement and spurred on by pressure from competing nation-states, Christopher Columbus lobbied for an expedition to establish a new trade route to Asia. With the fall of Constantinople to the Ottoman Turks, the land passage to the East had become a risky endeavor, and provisioning difficulties often beset merchants seeking spices, tea and opiates. After years of trying to persuade rulers in England, Spain, Portugal, Genoa and Venice to fund this venture, Columbus managed to convince King Ferdinand II of Aragon and Queen Isabella I of Castile whose union combined the two largest kingdoms in Spain to accept his proposal. Columbus' voyages to North America stimulated an era of increased trade and opened the ports of the New World to greatly expanded naval traffic. Individual colonies soon realized the necessity of setting beacons at important ports; the Spanish established a watchtower in the 1500s in St. Augustine that would become one of North America's earliest lighthouses.

England followed on Spain's heels, and the colony of Massachusetts erected a makeshift beacon to light Boston Harbor as early as 1673. Boston Light, the first official light station in the colonies that would become the United States, was built in 1716. After the Revolutionary War, the U.S. federal government took control of the nation's lighthouses, and new construction of these beacons began apace. Although lighthouse technology languished during tightfisted Stephen Pleasonton's more than three decades as fifth auditor of the U.S. treasury, the establishment of the Lighthouse Board, in 1852, assured the integration of important advancements, such as the Fresnel lens and construction plans that stressed longevity over penny-pinching.

Back in England, John Smeaton laid the groundwork for lighthouse innovations that would be taken up in the New World. In 1756 he began work on the third lighthouse at Eddystone, intended to warn sailors of treacherous rocks that had been the demise of many ships. Smeaton mastered the demands of the location, and his endeavor represented a huge

**▲ Christopher Columbus made** four trips to the New World. Between his third and fourth trips, Columbus and his brothers were arrested for supposed acts of torture used to govern Hispaniola. They were released after 6 weeks.

**◄◄ The Romans built the Tower** of Hercules in Spain in the second century AD. It is the oldest active lighthouse in the world. Legend has it that the light was built on the spot where Hercules slew the giant Geryon and then buried his head and weapons. The light appears above a skull and bones on the coat-of-arms of A Coruña.

**◄ This painting shows Christopher** Columbus and his crew landing in San Salvador on October 12, 1492, and claiming it for Spain.

leap forward in the development of lighthouse construction. The building crew, composed of Cornish tin miners, used hydraulic lime (which cures underwater) in conjunction with a system of dovetail joints to anchor the stones to the rock and each other. Modeled on an oak tree, with a wide base that tapered gradually, Smeaton's tower at Eddystone protected boats traveling past England's southwestern shores for more than 100 years.

Eddystone Light provided the blueprint for another engineering feat, this time at Inchcape, also known as the Bell Rock, located in the North Sea some 12 miles (19 km) east of the Scotland coast. Lighting this hazard posed seemingly insurmountable challenges, including total submersion of the rocks at high tide. The credit for the design of the tower often goes to Robert Stevenson, the onsite engineer who sired a lineage of master lighthouse builders, but

▸ **St. Augustine Lighthouse** was built in 1824 from the remains of a watchtower built in the 1500s. Not only is the light Florida's first lighthouse, but also it is the site of the oldest known aid to navigation in North America.

▾ **The original tower at Boston Harbor** was destroyed during the American Revolution and its replacement built in 1783. The current tower is the second oldest in the United States.

John Rennie made significant contributions to the plan as well. The tower, a jigsaw puzzle of sorts, was composed of courses of precisely cut interlocking granite or sandstone pieces. Twenty-four candles, each with a silvered parabolic reflector, rotated on a clockwork mechanism to illuminate Scotland's first revolving light. The 1811 tower stands today in testament to the innovative design and precise execution of the difficult undertaking at Bell Rock.

Modern lighthouses have drawn on all these improvements, and a variety of structures have been used to suit a particular lighthouse's unique circumstances. Screw-pile construction allows builders to erect lighthouses by drilling into the soft bottom of waterways and placing the signal on stilts above the waves. Caissons are utilized in colder waters where ice floes would damage the legs of the lighthouse. Texas towers, modeled on the oil-drilling platforms built off the coast of Texas, light ports and warn of hazards in the waters of Massachusetts, North Carolina, Georgia, Virginia and New York. Breakwater and pierhead lights shine at the end of long jetties, usually in lakes. Modern times find skeletal towers to be the most efficient and cost-effective choice for new lights, and large navigational buoys also serve to protect ships.

Many lighthouses were rendered obsolete by navigational developments, such as the Global Positioning System (GPS). Light stations were automated, and, without the care of keepers, the buildings began to deteriorate. The U.S. Coast Guard called for the demolition of several lighthouses that were no longer active aids to navigation. Although some lights were torn down, many local communities rose up in passionate support of their region's lighthouses. In 2000, the U.S. federal government passed the His-toric Lighthouse Preservation Act. Because of this legislation and the advocacy of millions of lighthouse fans, many of the lights that guided the vessels of our ancestors are now accessible to the public. Today light stations serve as cultural links between modern times and the past, and in this capacity these enduring beacons will continue to shine into the future.

◂◂ **After cracks appeared in the** rock used to build the third Eddystone Lighthouse, it was dismantled in 1882 and moved to Plymouth Hoe as tribute to the builder, John Smeaton.

▾ **The Middle Bay Lighthouse in** Alabama was built in 1885 in the middle of Mobile Bay. Constructed using screw piling, the light is currently under restoration after being deactivated in 1967.

# Conical & Cylindrical
## CONSTRUCTION

**THE STREAMLINED FORMS OF** conical and cylindrical towers withstand the ravages of the sea so effectively that they are among the most popular and enduring lighthouse shapes. Both types have a round cross-section, but conical lighthouses taper from a wide base at the bottom to a narrower diameter at the top. The summit and nadir of cylindrical lighthouses are nearly identical in diameter. Wind slips by the smooth walls of both shapes and doesn't exert as much pressure as on an angled construction. The walls of the towers are often many feet thick and can be made of stone, brick, plaster or iron.

◀ **Portland Head Lighthouse**
on Cape Elizabeth, Maine

# POINT ARENA

## *Light*

### California *(1870)*

▲ **Located 90 miles (145 km) north** of San Francisco, Point Arena is difficult to navigate due to its rapid currents, jagged reef and the arena rock which extends a mile into the Pacific.

▶ **The tallest lighthouse on** the West Coast, the Point Arena Lighthouse is the closest spot on the mainland to Hawaii, at a distance of 2,045 nautical miles.

*A* star of a lighthouse, Point Arena was featured in the 1982 film *Treasure,* as well as Mel Gibson's *Forever Young* in 1992. The tall tower, built by smokestack engineers, stretches up an impressive 115 feet (35 m) and affords visitors a bird's-eye view from the top. Point Arena Lighthouse is located directly above the San Andreas Fault. Movements at this uneasy juncture of tectonic plates destroyed the original lighthouse, as well as devastated nearby San Francisco in the 1906 earthquake. The current tower, completed in 1908, was the first steel-reinforced concrete lighthouse in the United States.

LOCATION: California
TOWER HEIGHT: 115 ft. (35 m)
FOCAL PLANE: 155 ft. (47 m)
DAYMARK: Cylindrical white concrete tower with black gallery and lantern
LIGHT CHARACTERISTICS: White flash every 15 seconds
SITE ESTABLISHED: 1870
CURRENT USE: Active

LOCATION: British Columbia
TOWER HEIGHT: 48 ft. (15 m)
FOCAL PLANE: 71 ft. (22 m)
DAYMARK: Round brick tower
with lantern and gallery
LIGHT CHARACTERISTICS:
White flash at 5-second
intervals
SITE ESTABLISHED: 1860
CURRENT USE: Active

# FISGARD

## *Light*

### British Columbia *(1860)*

▲ **Architect and contractor**
John Wright built the Fisgard Light and attached a keeper's residence and designed it to endure the severe weather of Vancouver Island.

◄ **The lighthouse's first keeper**
was the Englishman George Davies, who in 1859 brought the necessary lamps and machinery for the station's lantern room. Fisgard Light became automated 60 years later.

*F*isgard Lighthouse, erected by the British in 1859–1860, is the oldest light on the west coast of Canada. The beacon served as sentinel of the British Pacific squadron and now marks the home base of the Royal Canadian Navy. Fisgard and her sister station at Race Rocks guide vessels through the entrance of the Esquimalt Harbour, a port that boomed with trade in the wake of the Fraser gold rush. The light is an active aid to navigation, and the keeper's quarters house exhibits on lighthouses and local maritime history.

# YAQUINA HEAD

## *Light*
Oregon *(1871)*

One of the most visited lighthouses on the West Coast, Yaquina Head Light is located 3 miles (5 km) north of the entrance to Newport's Yaquina Bay. The outcropping of rock that provides the foundation to this notable tower is composed of magnetized iron that wreaks havoc on compasses that guide vessels through these waters. Since the completion of its construction in 1873, the lighthouse has steadied the course of shipping traffic with beams that reach 19 miles (31 km) out to sea. Yaquina Head Light has the distinction of being the tallest lighthouse tower in the state of Oregon.

**▲ The beacon can be seen** from the Pacific Coast Highway and is a popular destination point. It was especially so in the early 20th century. There were roughly 10,000 visitors in 1920 and 14,196 in 1931.

**▶ Although the keeper's house** and other structures from its original construction have been torn down, the current station includes an 1873 cistern and an 1889 oil house.

LOCATION: Oregon
TOWER HEIGHT: 93 ft. (28 m)
FOCAL PLANE: 162 ft. (49 m)
DAYMARK: Conical white tower, black lantern and trim, red lantern roof
LIGHT CHARACTERISTICS: Fixed white light
SITE ESTABLISHED: 1871
CURRENT USE: Active

▲ **A recent restoration effort has** focused on repairing and replacing the eroded cast iron pieces of the parapet and lantern roof, and new coats of white paint have enhanced the tower's exterior.

⚡ **The lighthouse was automated in** 1966, and a massive 12-foot (3.5 m) high first-order Fresnel lens still operates in the green and red lantern room. It is the only lighthouse in Oregon with a marble floor.

◀◀ **The tower had originally been** proposed for Cape Foulweather, a point farther north on Oregon's coast, but the construction crew mistakenly landed on Yaquina Head and erected the tower there instead. It took 1 year and 370,000 bricks to build the lighthouse.

▸ **Yaquina Head's light has been active** since its first head keeper, Fayette Crosby, climbed the tower's 114 steps to light the oil-burning wick on August 20, 1873.

◀ **In the 1930s Yaquina Head's** three-person crew was reduced to two, its power source was changed from whale oil to electricity, it received a new radio beacon, and its light pattern was changed from a fixed beam to a flashing signal.

▲ **The construction of Yaquina Head** was difficult to complete because the building site was located on a rocky crag, and materials had to be unloaded almost a mile away from the site and dragged up the cliff.

▶▶ **When struck by lightning in October** of 1920, the tower's only damage was a shearing away of the black paint on the handrail. The tower is within 1 inch (2.5 cm) of standing perfectly straight.

# PONCE DE LEON

## Light
### Florida *(1887)*

◀ **The original lighthouse**
was erected rapidly during the
Seminole Wars, but within 2 years,
erosion toppled the tower to the sand
dunes. Today Ponce de Leon stands
as the sole beacon in a 100-mile
(161 km) stretch of coast between
Saint Augustine and Cape Canaveral.

▲ **Although the Coast Guard**
deactivated the Ponce de Leon Light
in 1972, the tower was reinstated
in 1983 after a nearby lighthouse
proved ineffective. The beacon's
bright, flashing beam extends over
the Florida coastline and the Halifax
River at a range of 17 miles (27 km).

LOCATION: Florida
TOWER HEIGHT: 175 ft. (53 m)
FOCAL PLANE: 159 ft. (48 m)
DAYMARK: Conical painted red
brick tower, black lantern
LIGHT CHARACTERISTICS:
6 flashes every 20 seconds
SITE ESTABLISHED: 1887
CURRENT USE: Active

*S*oaring to 175 feet (53 m), the Ponce de Leon
Inlet Lighthouse ranks as the second tallest
lighthouse in the United States. The Mosquito and
Indian rivers empty into the waterway, making it a
key locale for trade. In 1830 local plantations called
for a lighthouse to aid in the transport of oranges,
rice and cotton to distant shores, and construction
began in 1835. Winslow Lewis was commissioned
to build the lighthouse, but like many of his other
construction projects, the hastily built, poorly
planned beacon soon succumbed to the ravages of
weather. More than a million bricks were used to
create the foundation, the inner walls and the outer
walls of the replacement tower, which did not see
completion until 1887. Beautifully restored and well
maintained, the current station houses exhibitions
of historical significance and offers visitors a rare
opportunity to view a revolving Fresnel lens at work.

◀◀ **Twelve-foot (3.5 m) thick concrete** walls form a foundation that is more than 40 feet (12 m) wide and support the soaring Ponce de Leon Light. The structure has endured a scores of roaring tempests and the massive earthquake of 1886.

▲ **The lighthouse's cast iron spiral** staircase has 203 steep steps — including the seven granite steps at its entrance — which lead to the balcony surrounding the lantern room.

LOCATION: Oregon
TOWER HEIGHT: 56 ft. (17 m)
FOCAL PLANE: 205 ft. (62 m)
DAYMARK: Conical white
stucco tower, green lantern,
red lantern roof
LIGHT CHARACTERISTICS:
White flash every 10 seconds
SITE ESTABLISHED: 1894
CURRENT USE: Active

*Light*
Oregon *(1894)*

▲ **Heceta Head Light is named** after Don Bruno de Heceta who undertook a secret voyage in 1775 for the Queen of Spain.

◄ **Standing on a bluff 150 feet** (46 m) above the ocean, the lighthouse has the strongest beam on Oregon's coast and can be viewed 21 miles (34 km) out to sea.

Heceta Head Lighthouse still uses its original first-order Fresnel lens and casts the strongest beam of any lighthouse on the Oregon coast, sending rays that reach 21 miles (34 km) out to sea. Both the lighthouse and the duplex that originally housed the first and second assistant lighthouse keepers are considered architecturally significant and are on the National Register of Historic Places. The construction cost the federal government $180,000, a colossal sum in the 1890s. The endeavor involved shipping materials to a drop-off point on the nearby Suislaw River and then carting supplies by mule to the steep bluff. A friendly ghost named Rue is said to wander the grounds, and visitors can hope to make her acquaintance while sojourning at the keeper's residence that has since been converted to a bed and breakfast.

# HECETA HEAD *Light*

▴ **Before 1894, the year that the** lighthouse was built, there was no light to steer ships off the coast of Oregon between Cape Foulweather and Cape Arago.

◂ **Heceta's light is a first-order** Fresnel lens crafted in England in 1894, and it originally rotated with the help of a weighted pendulum. Although the original lens is still in operation, today an automatic motor powers the light's movement.

▸▸ **Located only 2 miles (3 km)** away from Sea Lion Caves, the lighthouse stands in the middle of a 205-foot (62 m) tall promontory and is surrounded by Sitka spruce and shore pines.

LOCATION: Florida
TOWER HEIGHT: 145 ft. (44 m)
FOCAL PLANE: 137 ft. (42 m)
DAYMARK: Conical tower
with black and white bands,
black lantern
LIGHT CHARACTERISTICS:
2 white flashes 5 seconds apart,
20-second intervals
SITE ESTABLISHED: 1848
CURRENT USE: Active

*Light*

Florida *(1868)*

▲ **The striped beacon had to be** disassembled and moved farther inland due to sand erosion and the encroaching shoreline. Mules dragged the disassembled pieces along tram rails, and after 2 years, Cape Canaveral Light was relit in 1894.

◄ **The first Cape Canaveral** lighthouse was only 65 feet (20 m) tall, and its light was so weak that ships kept running aground on the ocean's rocky shoals. The new cast iron lighthouse was constructed after the Civil War and peers out over the Atlantic at more than twice the height of the original.

Although passage to the ironbound, brick lighthouse proved difficult, neighbors traveled over land and sea to get to the Lighthouse Balls at Cape Canaveral in the period following the Civil War. The newly moved and improved lighthouse completed in 1868 was equipped with a first-order Fresnel lens, as well as the only piano in the area. Lightkeeper Mills O. Burnham lived there with his wife and children and tended the light for 33 years. Since then, the beacon has seen the advent of the space age. It is rumored that Wernher von Braun watched the early launchings of his rockets from a walkway at the tower's top as they took off at Cape Canaveral. Quite close to the NASA launch site, the lighthouse is currently owned and maintained by the United States Air Force.

▲ **Cape Canaveral's earthshaking** rocket launches significantly damaged the tower's first-order Fresnel lens. Beginning in 1993, Cape Canaveral Light underwent a considerable restoration process, and in 1995 a DCB-224 Optic lens finally replaced the original. That same year the Coast Guard continued its repairs by exchanging the old lantern room for a newly modernized one.

◀◀ **In the late 1950s, the lighthouse** was often used as a forward observation point for the launch of missiles and rockets from Cape Canaveral's many seaside launch pads. Experiments of engineers and scientists from the Cape Canaveral Air Force station rocketed past the 145-foot (44 m) tall beacon of light.

▶ **The original roof and lantern** room are now on display as a gazebo at the Air Force Space and Missile Museum. The 1868 Fresnel lens is preserved at the Ayres Davies Lens Exhibit Building at the Ponce de Leon Lighthouse Museum.

**▸▸Portland Head sits perched** on the rocky headline of the Maine coastland guarding Casco Bay. The red-roofed keeper's house accompanies this monumental pinnacle.

**▾ Dedicated to the eminent** Revolutionary War general Marquis de Lafayette, Portland Head was the first major project tackled by the U.S. federal government in the late 18th century. President George Washington took interest and advised Congress to make the lighthouse a priority.

LOCATION: Maine
TOWER HEIGHT: 80 ft. (24 m)
FOCAL PLANE: 101 ft. (31 m)
DAYMARK: Conical painted white brick tower, black lantern
LIGHT CHARACTERISTICS: Flashing white light at 4-second intervals
SITE ESTABLISHED: 1791
CURRENT USE: Active

# PORTLAND HEAD

*Light*

Maine *(1791)*

A favorite haunt of poet Henry Wadsworth Longfellow, the sentinel at Portland Head provided inspiration for his poem "The Lighthouse." The structure, originally built in 1791, has undergone myriad transformations: 20 feet (6 m) were added to the tower's height and a second-order Fresnel lens was installed in 1864, following the wreck of the *Bohemian*. With the advent of a new lighthouse at Halfway Rock, the Portland station was deemed less important. The tower was shortened again, and the second-order lens downgraded to a weaker, fourth-order Fresnel. After complaints, the tower was restored to its former height in 1885. Despite its ups and downs, the light at Portland Head continues to endure stormy seas and steadfastly lights the way to the busy seaport.

**▲ In 1885 the tower's interior** circular stairway was built of wrought iron. It extends up the 105-foot (32 m) tall beacon whose light can be seen for 24 nautical miles.

**◀ The keeper who worked longest** at Portland Head Light was Captain Joshua Strout, who spent 35 years tending the light along with his parrot, Billy. His son, Joseph, replaced him and kept the station in order for 20 more years.

**◀◀ Cape Elizabeth's Portland Head** sits on the shores of Fort Williams Park. It was the first lighthouse built on Maine's coast and the 13th lighthouse ever erected in the United States.

▲ **In February 1972 a ruthless** squall tore the 2,000-pound (907 kg) fog bell from the tower, ripped out 80 feet (24 m) of steel fence, broke a 25-foot (8 m) high window, and covered the lighthouse station "foot deep in mud and flotsam, including starfish."

◀ **During World War II,** Portland Head's light went dark for 3 years. In 1958, after the station was electrified, aerobeacons replaced the fourth-order Fresnel lens.

▶▶ **One of the 60 lighthouses of** Maine, Portland Head's last keeper was Robert Thayer, who authored *Lighthouses of the Maine Coast and the Men Who Keep Them*. The Coast Guard staffed the station until 1989 when the light became automated.

LOCATION: Rhode Island
TOWER HEIGHT: 34 ft. (10 m)
FOCAL PLANE: 40 ft. (12 m)
DAYMARK: Conical structure
with white top, granite bottom
and black lantern
LIGHT CHARACTERISTICS:
Red light — 3 seconds on,
3 seconds off
SITE ESTABLISHED: 1890
CURRENT USE: Active

*Light*

**Rhode Island** *(1890)*

▲**Gazing over Narragansett Bay's** East Passage, Castle Hill Light initially rested upon a cove, but the hurricane of 1938 converted the rocky beach to an island. The storm also tore down the original keeper's dwelling, which was never rebuilt.

◄ **The granite structure built into** the face of a cliff assists maritime ships on their way to Newport and Providence. The beacon often marks the start and finish of Newport yacht races.

The land at Castle Hill was sold to the federal government by oceanographer, naturalist and zoologist Alexander Agassiz for the token amount of $1. However low his asking price, he cost the project dearly in time when he refused to allow the contractor to cross his property to access the location for the light. The Lighthouse Board and Agassiz finally came to an agreement, and the station was completed in 1890. The fog bell installed at the light was the source of more contention. Agassiz complained that the noise from the 1,300-pound (590 kg) bell was intolerable. A sound screen between the light and Agassiz's property became the eventual solution. The granite sentinel stands 34 feet (10 m) tall, and its endurance is a testament to the skill of Henry Hobson Richardson, who is believed to have designed the structure.

# BODIE ISLAND

## *Light*

### North Carolina *(1872)*

▲ **Built in the classic conical design** with Victorian detailing, Bodie Island Light guards the North Carolina shores of the Atlantic, including the infamous "Graveyard of the Atlantic."

▸ **The first two "Bodie Island"** lighthouses had been built on the south side of the Oregon Inlet on Pea Island. The 15-acre property, purchased by the government for $150 in 1846, was north of the inlet.

The first station at Bodie Island suffered from the incompetence and penny-pinching that was the signature of the fifth auditor of the Treasury. The unsupported foundation of the structure quickly became unstable, and the tower leaned increasingly off plumb. Within 11 years it was demolished. Its successor also met with an early demise when Confederate troops blew it up in an effort to sabotage the British occupation of North Carolina. In 1872, Dexter Stetson, having recently completed the Cape Hatteras Light, brought his expertise to bear on the construction of the final tower at Bodie Island. He employed his innovative method of driving timber pilings below ground to create a secure foundation in shifting sands. The work has held up admirably, and this last version of the Bodie Island Light shines on in the care of the National Park Service, as a private aid to navigation.

LOCATION: North Carolina
TOWER HEIGHT: 170 ft. (52 m)
FOCAL PLANE: 156 ft. (48 m)
DAYMARK: Made of brick, cast iron and stone painted with white and black bands and a black lantern
LIGHT CHARACTERISTICS: 2 white flashes every 30 seconds
SITE ESTABLISHED: 1848
CURRENT USE: Active

**The first keepers of the light led** isolated lives on the undeveloped island. The nearest village was the neighboring Roanoke Island, a destination only accessible by boat.

▸ **A year after the tower was** constructed, a flock of geese crashed into the first-order Fresnel lens, severely damaging it. A screen was soon fitted to prevent further mishaps.

▾ **In 1932 the light was automated,** and in 1953 the station was transferred to the protection of the National Park Service.

LOCATION: Newfoundland
TOWER HEIGHT: 36 ft. (11 m)
FOCAL PLANE: 166 ft. (51 m)
DAYMARK: Cylindrical stone
tower with lantern painted red
with white stripes
LIGHT CHARACTERISTICS: None
SITE ESTABLISHED: 1843
CURRENT USE: Inactive

*Light*

Newfoundland *(1873)*

▲ **Newfoundland's Cape Bonavista** showcases an impressive birdcage-style lantern that sits atop the keeper's house. The lighthouse's 16-mirror-lamp-and-reflector optic had formerly been in use at Bell Rock Light in Scotland.

◀ **The lighthouse was constructed** for the purpose of guiding mariners — bound for Labrador — over Newfoundland's rocky coastline. In 1843 the first lighting apparatus was a revolving red and white catoptric light that was composed of 16 Argand burners.

$\mathcal{L}$egend has it that when John Cabot first saw land after his voyage across the Atlantic in 1497, he looked at the cape on the eastern coast of Newfoundland and cried *"Buona vista!"* Although there is some wrangling over whether the cape was indeed his first foray onto dry land, there can be no question about the beauty of the view at Cape Bonavista. The tower was built in 1873 and rises out of a keeper's dwelling that has been traditionally painted with red and white vertical stripes. The light and lens have been transferred to a skeletal tower nearby, which currently serves as the navigational aid for the area, and the old station houses a museum with historic artifacts from the lighthouse's early days.

# CAPE LOOKOUT

## *Light*

### North Carolina *(1859)*

$S$ailors in the first half of the 19th century complained that they were more likely to run aground looking for the weak light at Cape Lookout than be aided by its rays. The second tower, erected at the cape in 1859, greatly improved matters. Built of red brick and still an active aid to navigation today, the tower rises 169 feet (52 m), and its light is visible 19 miles (31 km) out to sea, enabling it to effectively warn boats of the hazards of the Outer Banks. The lens was damaged and the light darkened during the battles of the Civil War. After the war ended, many repairs were made and cast iron steps replaced the rotten wooden stairs. In 1873 the new keeper's quarters were completed, and the tower was painted with its signature black and white diamonds. Some say that this pattern was originally intended for Hatteras, to indicate proximity to the Diamond Shoals, but because of a mix-up it was painted on the light at Cape Lookout instead.

**The first Cape Lookout Lighthouse** of 1812 had interior walls made of brick and an outer layer of wood painted with red and white stripes. Even though it cost the extravagant amount of $20,678 to build, its light was very weak, earning it the nickname of "Horrible Headland."

**One of the five lighthouses on** the string of islands referred to as the Outer Banks of North Carolina, the black and white beacon guides vessels safely through the Cape Lookout shoals.

LOCATION: North Carolina
TOWER HEIGHT: 169 ft. (52 m)
FOCAL PLANE: 156 ft. (48 m)
DAYMARK: Checkered black and white diamond
LIGHT CHARACTERISTICS: White flash every 15 seconds
SITE ESTABLISHED: 1812
CURRENT USE: Active

**▲ Still in operation today,**
the lighthouse became automated in
1950 and uses a DCB-24 optic lens
that shines over the four barrier islands
of North Carolina from Ocracoke to
Beaufort Inlet.

**▶ The coast of the Outer Banks is**
notoriously dangerous — more than
600 ships have sunk; hidden reefs
extend for 14 miles (23 km) out into the
Atlantic, and rapid currents relentlessly
shift the shallow sandbars.

**▶▶ Accompanying the tower are**
a two-story brick keeper's house from
1873, a brick oil house, a coal shed,
two cisterns, a summer kitchen and
a stable.

LOCATION: New York
TOWER HEIGHT: 168 ft. (51 m)
FOCAL PLANE: 180 ft. (55 m)
DAYMARK: Conical structure
with four black and white bands
LIGHT CHARACTERISTICS:
White flash every 7.5 seconds
SITE ESTABLISHED: 1827
CURRENT USE: Active

# FIRE ISLAND

## *Light*

### New York *(1827)*

**The tapered tower was given** a flared base to increase its stability and a coal-fired power plant was added in the late 19th century. It is rumored that rum runners during prohibition used the lighthouse to navigate the Fire Island inlet.

**The first lighthouse on** Fire Island was only 74 feet (23 m) tall, while the new beacon is more than twice that height. Locals fondly call its rapidly flashing light the "Winking Woman."

The Lighthouse Board, shortly after it was formed in 1852, declared the light at Fire Island inadequate. The new tower, erected in 1858, was almost double the height of the original, and its white light shone through a first-order Fresnel lens. In 1894 this light was considered extremely important to transatlantic steamers headed to New York. The vessels set their course by the beacon because it was often the first light that they could see. By 1981 the neglected tower was declared unsafe and was scheduled for demolition. This plan aroused the community to action, and the Fire Island Lighthouse Preservation Society came into the fray. The society raised $1 million to restore and protect the building and currently maintains the light as a private aid to navigation.

# CAPE NEDDICK

## *Light*

### Maine *(1879)*

Cape Neddick Light, known as the Nubble, is located on Nubble Island off the coast of Maine. So many vessels foundered on this outcropping of rock when sailing to York Harbor that in 1879, the federal government erected a cast iron, brick-lined station to warn ships of the hazard. The tower could be accessed through a covered walkway from the keeper's quarters in inclement weather. Former keepers traveled over sandbars to the mainland at low tide, but this is currently considered too dangerous a practice for visitors. On a clear day, the vantage point from the top of the Nubble affords a view of Boon Lighthouse, which is more than 6 miles (10 km) away.

**The beacon has witnessed** many rescue operations, including the miraculous moment when keeper Fairfield Moore saved a captain and his son whose ship, the *Robert W*, was wrecked on treacherous submerged rocks.

**Cape Neddick Light stands 88** feet (27 m) above sea level and its former 3,000-pound (1,361 kg) fog bell could at one time be heard by the Boon Island keepers, more than 6 miles (10 km) away.

LOCATION: Maine
TOWER HEIGHT: 41 ft. (12 m)
FOCAL PLANE: 88 ft. (27 m)
DAYMARK: Cylindrical structure painted white with a black lantern
LIGHT CHARACTERISTICS: Red light — 3 seconds on, 3 seconds off
SITE ESTABLISHED: 1879
CURRENT USE: Active

LOCATION: California
TOWER HEIGHT: 115 ft. (35 m)
FOCAL PLANE: 148 ft. (45 m)
DAYMARK: Conical structure
attached to a workroom
painted white with black trim
LIGHT CHARACTERISTICS:
White flash every 10 seconds
SITE ESTABLISHED: 1871
CURRENT USE: Active

*Light*

California *(1871)*

▲ **The lantern room displays a** first-order Fresnel lens with 1,008 prisms, which stands 16 feet (5 m) tall and weights 4 tons. The lens had previously been in use at Cape Hatteras Light before it was shipped to California.

◄ **Pigeon Point Light was** originally known as Punta de las Balenas (Whale Point). Fifty miles (80 km) south of San Francisco, the 115-foot (35 m) tower can be seen for miles away on U.S. Highway 1.

𝒫igeon Point was named for the clipper ship *Carrier Pigeon*, which met its demise on the rocky outcropping in 1853. Three subsequent shipwrecks in the 1860s persuaded Congress to approve a lighthouse at the spot. The tower, built in 1871, shares the honor of being the tallest lighthouse on the West Coast with the California's Point Arena Lighthouse. The intertidal zone just off the shore supports a great variety of life, including pods of gray whales that migrate through the area in late winter to early spring.

# NED'S POINT

## Light

**Massachusetts** *(1837)*

Legend has it that Ned's Point Lighthouse got off to a rocky start. Commissioned with the support of then congressman John Quincy Adams the lighthouse experienced a number of delays. The contractor, besides being a shipbuilder and running a salt works, managed a local tavern where he would reportedly lure inspectors to buy time when construction fell behind schedule. Early inspections of the lighthouse testify to a multitude of leaks that even extinguished the light in the lantern from time to time. Improvements such as a new lantern and replacement of old mortar have shored up any failings in the structure. The original tower, completed in 1838, still stands today.

LOCATION: Massachusetts
TOWER HEIGHT: 39 ft. (12 m)
FOCAL PLANE: 41 ft. (12 m)
DAYMARK: Conical white stone tower with black lantern and gallery
LIGHT CHARACTERISTICS: White light — 3 seconds on, 3 seconds off
SITE ESTABLISHED: 1837
CURRENT USE: Active

**◄◄ Thirty-two cantilevered granite** stairs ascend to the octagonal-shaped lantern room, which was originally beehive-shaped and only 5 feet 8 inches (170 cm) high. The lighthouse's beam shines 41 feet (12 m) above sea level.

**▾ The celebrated beacon rests** at the entrance of Mattapoisett Harbor overlooking Buzzard's Bay. The stones that compose the tower were all hand-cut and the cost of construction was a mere $450.

**Plans to erect a lighthouse** on Cape Hatteras began as early as 1792. The original design described the tower as 90 feet (27 m) tall and used whale oil as fuel. The light proved too weak, and the current Victorian-styled tower is more than twice the former one's height.

**The painter who was assigned** the task of painting Cape Hatteras is rumored to have mixed up the design plans, and the diamonds, appropriate for warning ships of the Diamond Shoals, went to Cape Lookout. The spiral zebra-striping coated the Hatteras' tower.

# Light

## North Carolina *(1803)*

LOCATION: North Carolina
TOWER HEIGHT: 200 ft. (61 m)
FOCAL PLANE: 193 ft. (59 m)
DAYMARK: Conical tower with black and white spiral stripes, black lantern and gallery
LIGHT CHARACTERISTICS: White flash every 7.5 seconds
SITE ESTABLISHED: 1803
CURRENT USE: Active

Extending 14 miles (23 km) off the coast of Cape Hatteras lie the Diamond Shoals — shifting sandbars that have caused the demise of more than 600 ships. It is here that the sunny Gulf Stream and the frigid Labrador Current converge to create big swells and dangerous winds. The original light at Cape Hatteras, completed in 1803, was so weak that other ships mistook it for a steamer. Dubbed a "wretched light" by a Navy inspector in 1851, it was replaced by the 193-foot (59 m) tall tower capable of beaming 24 miles (39 km) out to sea. The current structure is the tallest lighthouse in the United States and has warned ships of the treacherous "Graveyard of the Atlantic" since 1871. When the rising Atlantic and years of erosion jeopardized the foundation of the lighthouse, local organizations raised funds and moved the massive brick edifice farther inland, where it is at least temporarily safe from encroaching waters.

▲ **At the time it was built,**
Cape Hatteras was the tallest
lighthouse in the world. Its light,
replaced in 1972 with a DCB-24
lens, is visible every 7 seconds.

◀ **During the Civil War,**
Confederate troops dismantled
Cape Hatteras' Fresnel lens to
keep the Union's navy at bay.
The lens was then shipped to
Paris for repairs and returned
to the lighthouse in 1870.

# CAPE HATTERAS *Light*

▲ **Nicknamed "The Big Barber Pole,"** the beacon was constructed with 1,250,000 bricks baked in kilns on the banks of the James River in Virginia.

▶ **Supporting the 6,250-ton** lighthouse are the red-brick base's walls, with 14 feet (4 m) of solid masonry and a foundation of granite and pine timber.

▶▶ **An expansive Atlantic view** is visible from the top of Cape Hatteras, but the climb is extremely challenging. A total of 268 steps compose the spiral staircase — a height equal to walking up 12 flights of stairs.

# CAPE ANN

## *Light*

### Massachusetts *(1771)*

$\mathcal{T}$he only currently operating twin lights in the nation, the Cape Ann station has woven its place into U.S. history — from its dark days during the Revolutionary War when Tory keeper Captain Kirkwood was forcibly expelled — to the horn blast that warned President Woodrow Wilson's steamer of impending disaster in 1919. The twin lights are located on an island three-quarters of a mile off the coast of Rockport, Massachusetts. The island was named for Anthony Thatcher, whose vessel, the *Watch and Wait*, was wrecked on the shores of the island during a violent hurricane in 1635. Twenty-one of the passengers, including Thatcher's four children, perished in the wreck. The only ones to survive the storm were Thatcher and his wife, Elizabeth.

▲ **Known as "Thatcher's Woe"** in remembrance of the catastrophic shipwreck, Cape Ann is among the oldest lighthouses on the New England coast. It was the last lighthouse to be founded during the Colonial era.

▸ **The twin lighthouses of Thatcher** Island have been in operation since 1771 and peer out over the coasts of Cape Ann at 160 feet (49 m) above the sea.

LOCATION: Massachusetts
TOWER HEIGHT: 124 ft. (38 m)
FOCAL PLANE: 166 ft. (51 m)
DAYMARK: Twin conical granite towers, each with a lantern and gallery
LIGHT CHARACTERISTICS: Red flash every 5 seconds in south tower/fixed yellow light in north tower
SITE ESTABLISHED: 1771
CURRENT USE: Active

LOCATION: Massachusetts
TOWER HEIGHT: 89 ft. (27 m)
FOCAL PLANE: 102 ft. (31 m)
DAYMARK: Conical white tower, black lantern
LIGHT CHARACTERISTICS: White flash every 10 seconds
SITE ESTABLISHED: 1715
CURRENT USE: Active

**The first keeper of the lighthouse** was George Worthylake, who drowned along with his wife and daughter when they were returning to the island's shores in 1718.

**Resting on the rocky south** point of Little Brewster Island, Boston Harbor Light is 89 feet (27 m) tall and is the only lighthouse to be actively staffed by the Coast Guard.

*Light*

## Massachusetts *(1783)*

The first lighthouse in America, Boston Harbor light played a key role as the revolutionaries wrested control of the colonies from the British. The initial tower, erected in 1715, was paid for by the colony of Massachusetts Bay and maintained by taxes on vessels entering and leaving the harbor. After the Sons of Liberty tossed 342 chests of tea overboard to protest the British tea tax, the British navy blockaded the harbor and seized the lighthouse. General Washington retaliated by sending minutemen, who set fire to the lighthouse tower twice. Just as Washington's troops regained control of the area, the fleeing British exploded the remains of the battered beacon. In 1783 builders completed a new tower, and its light still pierces the night sky of the Massachusetts Bay.

▾ **The 800-foot (244 m) long Little** Brewster Island houses a white clapboard keeper's dwelling, an oil house and a fog signal building that all surround the Boston Harbor Light.

# WIND POINT

*Light*

Wisconsin *(1880)*

At the northern end of Racine Harbor sits Wisconsin's Wind Point Light, designed by General Orlando Metcalf Poe. Before the lighthouse was officially established, a lone tree was the only navigational marker on this portion of the southwest shore of Lake Michigan. The 108-foot (33 m) tower has four arched windows under the gallery and a 10-sided cast iron lantern. Besides operating as a beacon for ship captains, Wind Point Lighthouse and its keeper's quarters have served the community as a village hall and police headquarters since 1964. In that same year, the light was automated and the Fresnel lens was replaced by a DCB 24R.

◄ **One of the tallest and oldest** lighthouses active on the Great Lakes, the bright white tower has 144 steps and soars above all trees and buildings that surround it.

▶ **After 3 years of construction,** Wind Point Light was completed in 1880. It has guided vessels across the treacherous Racine Shoals with a beaming light that is visible for a distance of 19 miles (31 km).

LOCATION: Wisconsin
TOWER HEIGHT: 108 ft. (33 m)
FOCAL PLANE: 111 ft. (34 m)
DAYMARK: Conical white tower with black lantern and gallery
LIGHT CHARACTERISTICS: White flash every 20 seconds
SITE ESTABLISHED: 1877
CURRENT USE: Active

LOCATION: Maine
TOWER HEIGHT: 30 ft. (9 m)
FOCAL PLANE: 100 ft. (30 m)
DAYMARK: Cylindrical white
tower, black lantern and gallery
LIGHT CHARACTERISTICS:
Fixed white light
SITE ESTABLISHED: 1826
CURRENT USE: Active

# *Light*

## Maine *(1826)*

Anchored to a promontory whose craggy face was thought to resemble an owl, Owl's Head Light stands just 30 feet (9 m) tall. The cliff's elevation makes up for the tower's diminutive height, and the light shines at 100 feet (30 m) above sea level to guide boats into Rockland Harbor. Tales of romance and heroism abound here: lovers who were shipwrecked and frozen together, valiant dogs preventing disaster and deceased lighthouse keepers that come back to polish the brass. In 2007 former residents of the lighthouse, Paul and Mary Ellen Dilger, spearheaded an effort of the American Lighthouse Foundation to begin a complete restoration of this notable light.

**▲ Samuel de Champlain visited the** cape in 1605 when it was known as Bedabedec Point, "Cape of the Winds." The temperamental gales have often caused vessels to run aground on the submerged rocks. One schooner in 1850 was smashed to pieces, though the lighthouse's keeper managed to rescue its shipwrecked crew.

**◀ Overlooking Rockland Harbor on the** west side of Penobscot Bay, Owl's Head Light commands a breathtaking view of Rockland Breakwater Light. Both lights illuminate Maine's waterfront.

# ● OWL'S HEAD *Light*

▲ **In 1825 U.S. President**
John Quincy Adams sanctioned
the building of Owl's Head Light. In
1989 the station became one of the
last in the country to be automated.

◄ **Owl's Head Light's**
commanding fog signal guides
incoming crafts. In the 1930s the
keeper's springer spaniel, Spot,
was taught to pull on the fog-bell
rope whenever he heard a fleet
approaching.

▸ **The beacon's cylindrical tower**
with a black lantern has a fourth-
order Fresnel lens that replaced the
original lamps and reflectors
in 1856.

# THREE SISTERS

Dangerous sandbars off the coast of Nauset prompted the construction of three identical brick towers, 150 feet (46 m) apart in 1837. The idea was that the light station be distinguishable from nearby lighthouses, the twin lights at Chatham and the single at North Truro. The Three Sisters, as the new towers built by low-bidder Winslow Lewis were called, came under criticism for being poorly constructed. The project overseer claimed that the masons repeatedly used sand instead of mortar and laid the bricks randomly. In 1892 three movable wooden towers replaced the brick edifices that gave way to erosion, but these new lights were eventually sold off and used as private summer cottages. In 1975 the National Park Service acquired and reunited the trio, and they stand near the present single light that went into service in 1911 at Nauset Station.

▸▸**Due to the increasing threat of** erosion, in 1996 the still-active Nauset Light had to be moved 336 (102 m) feet farther from its old beach site.

▾ **The trio of conical brick towers'** nickname, "The Three Sisters of Nauset," is said to have originated because the lighthouses looked like women wearing black hats and white dresses.

## *Lights*

Massachusetts *(1837)*

LOCATION: Massachusetts
TOWER HEIGHT: 29 ft. (9 m)
FOCAL PLANE: 22 ft. (7 m)
DAYMARK: 3 identical conical white towers with black lantern
LIGHT CHARACTERISTICS: None
SITE ESTABLISHED: 1837
CURRENT USE: Inactive

# GAY HEAD

## Light

### Massachusetts (1799)

*Of all the heavenly phenomena that I have had the good fortune to witness — borealis lights, mock suns or meteoric showers — I have never seen anything that, in mystic splendor, equaled the trick of the magic lantern of Gay Head.*

— General David Hunter,
*Harper's Magazine,* 1853

In 1852, after being ranked the ninth most important seacoast light in the nation, the Gay Head station won the miracle that awed Hunter — a first-order Fresnel lens, composed of 1,008 prisms. This innovative optic would greatly increase the efficacy of lighthouses around the world. Anchored to the colorful striped clay cliffs that allow it to shine 170 feet (52 m) above sea level, the light is the oldest on Martha's Vineyard and can reach an amazing 25 miles (40 km) out to sea.

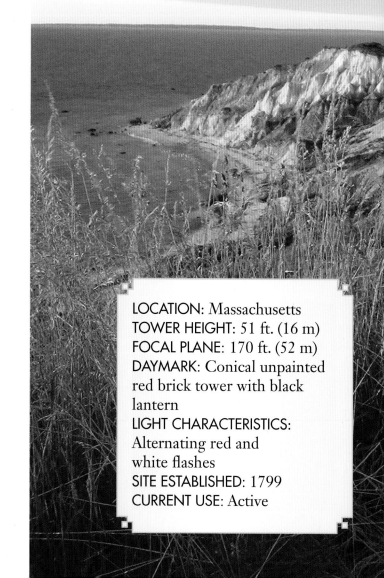

LOCATION: Massachusetts
TOWER HEIGHT: 51 ft. (16 m)
FOCAL PLANE: 170 ft. (52 m)
DAYMARK: Conical unpainted red brick tower with black lantern
LIGHT CHARACTERISTICS: Alternating red and white flashes
SITE ESTABLISHED: 1799
CURRENT USE: Active

◀◀ **The constant maritime traffic** of Vineyard Sound and the perilous submerged rock known as Devil's Bridge prompted Massachusetts state senator Peleg Coffin of Nantucket to call for a lighthouse to be built at Gay Head.

▼ **Gay Head is one of three** lighthouses on the island, including Edgartown and East Chop, and they are all maintained by the Martha's Vineyard Historical Society.

# GAY HEAD *Light*

◁ **In 1884 the lighthouse** witnessed one of the worst maritime accidents in New England history when the passenger ferry *City of Columbus* ran aground on Devil's Bridge, killing almost 100 passengers.

▶▶ **The conical brick lighthouse** stands perilously close to the eroding 130-foot (40 m) colored clay cliffs of Martha's Vineyard.

▽ **The first light erected at Gay** Head was a 47-foot (14 m) octagonal wooden lighthouse. Its keeper, Ebenezer Skiff, was the first white man to live in Gay Head, which was populated by Wampanoag Indians.

LOCATION: Maine
TOWER HEIGHT: 49 ft. (15 m)
FOCAL PLANE: 83 ft. (25 m)
DAYMARK: Cylindrical white and red striped tower, black lantern, red lantern roof
LIGHT CHARACTERISTICS: 2 white flashes every 15 seconds
SITE ESTABLISHED: 1808
CURRENT USE: Active

**The lighthouse station's** foghorn, located in a nearby brick building, has an electric eye that is able to sense when the air is thick with fog.

**Perched on a 40-foot (12 m)** cliff, West Quoddy Head gazes across the Bay of Fundy toward Canada's Campobello Island. It is one of Maine's earliest lighthouse stations.

**At the same time the** West Quoddy Head was erected, a one-and-a-half-story Victorian keeper's house was built. The original rubble-stone lighthouse was demolished and rebuilt in 1858.

Located on the easternmost point of the contiguous United States, West Quoddy Head Lighthouse has guided fishing and trade vessels through the swift currents of the windy and constricted passage of Quoddy Narrows since 1808. Over time the lighthouse was equipped with a fog cannon, a 4,000-pound (1,814 kg) bell, and a Daboll trumpet fog whistle to assist ships muddled by the frequent mists in the nearby Bay of Fundy. In 1858 the current tower was built and painted with the signature eight red and seven white "candy stripes."

*Light*

Maine *(1858)*

**▲ A 50-step spiral stairway extends** up the 49-foot (15 m) red-brick tower. The stairs become exceptionally steep as they reach the top and are met with a 10-rung ladder.

**▶▶ The tower's light, a third-order** Fresnel lens, was installed at the time of the tower's construction. It can be seen from a distance of up to 18 nautical miles.

# MORRIS ISLAND

## *Light*

### South Carolina *(1767)*

▲ **The original lighthouse was** constructed 1,200 feet (366 m) from the shore on Morris Island. Today the beacon is completely surrounded by Charleston Harbor and continues to be at risk of collapse.

▶ **In 1938 the Morris Island** Lighthouse was automated and the Fresnel lens was replaced. A sheet-steel bulkhead was placed around the bottom of the light to protect it from further erosion.

As early as 1673, settlers hung an open iron basket of fire as a navigational aid to boats entering the Charleston Harbor. The lighthouse at Morris Island, established in 1767 when George III still ruled the 13 colonies, improved on this technology and was among the first operational light beacons in the nation. The tower went dark during periods of the Revolutionary War, and was taken over by the new Congress, along with all other existing navigational aids. When South Carolina seceded from the union in 1860, it seized all the lights on the coast. Eventually, the battles that raged in Charleston completely destroyed the lighthouse. Erosion and an earthquake threatened the new tower built on the site, but an organization called Save the Light is fighting to protect and restore this historic monument.

LOCATION: South Carolina
TOWER HEIGHT: 161 ft. (49 m)
FOCAL PLANE: 158 ft. (48 m)
DAYMARK: Conical tower with weathered black and white bands, black lantern
LIGHT CHARACTERISTICS: None
SITE ESTABLISHED: 1767
CURRENT USE: Inactive

▲ **Inactive since 1962, the** 161-foot (49 m) brick tower stands atop a concrete foundation 8 feet (2.5 m) thick and extends 50 feet (15 m) into the seafloor. Its sturdy support system kept the light operational during the Charleston earthquake of 1885.

▸▸**In order to rescue the lighthouse** from demolition, Save the Light bought the lighthouse in 1999 for $75,000. The organization hopes to transfer its ownership of the Morris Island Light to the Heritage Trust Program of South Carolina, which is responsible for preserving the state's natural and historic areas.

LOCATION: California
TOWER HEIGHT: 40 ft. (12 m)
FOCAL PLANE: 277 ft. (84 m)
DAYMARK: Cylindrical white
concrete tower with black trim
and black lantern
LIGHT CHARACTERISTICS:
2 white flashes with 15-second
intervals every 60 seconds
SITE ESTABLISHED: 1912
CURRENT USE: Active

# ANACAPA ISLAND

## *Light*
### California *(1932)*

▲ **Fixed at the top of a 39-foot** (12 m) concrete cylindrical tower, a solar-powered acrylic lens replaced the third-order Fresnel lens in the 1980s.

◀◀ **After the steamer *Liebre* ran** ashore on the east coast of the Anacapa Island due to foggy conditions, there was a petition to build the last major light station on the West Coast.

*I*n 1853, the highly publicized shipwreck of the *Winfield Scott* sent gold rushers' newfound riches to the bottom of the sea. In the wake of this tragedy, President Franklin Pierce ordered that Anacapa Island, a chain of three adjacent islets, be reserved to build a lighthouse. After surveying the steep, perpendicular cliffs of volcanic rock, the U.S. Coast Guard pronounced the site "inconceivable for a lighthouse" since it was "inaccessible by any natural means." Numerous expensive groundings of marine vessels convinced the Lighthouse Bureau otherwise, and in 1932 construction was finally completed on the last major lighthouse to be built on the West Coast.

# ADMIRALTY HEAD

## *Light*
### Washington *(1861)*

$\mathcal{A}$dmiralty Head Lighthouse was one of the Pacific coast's first important navigational aids. Construction on the original red, wooden lighthouse was finished shortly before the beginning of the Civil War, and its light guided many vessels through Admiralty Inlet to the shores of Whidbey Island. The lighthouse's position was considered so strategically significant to the protection of Puget Sound that it was torn down and relocated during the Spanish Civil War to accommodate Fort Casey and the massive guns of the "triangle of fire," a trio of forts set up in the sound to deter enemy invasions. The present Spanish colonial–style structure stands 127 feet (39 m) above the water, and it was the last brick lighthouse designed by acclaimed architect Carl Leick.

LOCATION: Washington
TOWER HEIGHT: 30 ft. (9 m)
FOCAL PLANE: 127 ft. (39 m)
DAYMARK: Conical white
stucco tower with black lantern
and gallery
LIGHT CHARACTERISTICS: None
SITE ESTABLISHED: 1861
CURRENT USE: Inactive

◀◀ **One of the earliest navigational**
markers on the West Coast,
Admiralty Head sits atop Red Bluff,
and its fixed white light's beam
directs Puget Sound marine traffic up
to 16 miles (26 km) away.

▼ **The new lighthouse of 1903**
was deactivated in 1927, when
it became a residence for officers
stationed at Fort Casey. Today the
lighthouse and Spanish-styled house
are a historic museum.

LOCATION: Washington
TOWER HEIGHT: 53 ft. (16 m)
FOCAL PLANE: 220 ft. (67 m)
DAYMARK: Conical white stone
tower with black horizontal
band and black lantern
LIGHT CHARACTERISTICS:
Alternating red and white
flashes every 15 seconds
SITE ESTABLISHED: 1856
CURRENT USE: Active

◀ **Fur trader John Meares confused** the headland of the cape for another landfall farther south and sailed away on his ship in disappointment, thereby giving the cape its name.

▲ **The station sits close to** Fort Canby, a military reservation established in 1852 to protect the entrance of the Columbia River. The reverberations from the post's substantial artillery range have been known to shatter the lighthouse's windows.

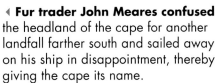

*Light*

Washington *(1856)*

$\mathcal{K}$nown as the Graveyard of the Pacific, the treacherous area at the mouth of the Columbia River has drowned almost 2,000 vessels in the last 300 years. This region harbors a deadly river bar and powerful currents. The light at Cape Disappointment greatly lessened the dangers, even though its construction was fraught with difficulty. The first ship bearing materials for the lighthouse foundered on the shores of the cape. Although a second ship brought more supplies, once the tower was constructed, workers discovered that it was too small to accommodate the 4-ton first-order Fresnel lens assigned to the station. The lighthouse was taken apart brick by brick, rebuilt, and finally lit in 1856. It is the oldest operating light on the Pacific coast.

**Joel Munson, one of the first keepers of** Cape Disappointment, arrived at the station in 1865. Munson raised money to buy a lifesaving boat for the station. His efforts proved successful when the *W. B. Scranton* crashed on the sandbar and Munson's boat rescued the crew.

**The 53-foot (16 m) conical tower was first** lit on October 15, 1856. In 1898 the lens was exchanged for a fourth-order Barbier & Bernard lens that is still in use. Its red and white flashes continue to guide vessels away from harm.

**Builders took three years to complete** the lighthouse, slowed by the cape's shallow sandbars and rocky shoreline. One of the vessels carrying supplies and materials for the light was wrecked on the rocks during rough conditions.

# ST. AUGUSTINE

## *Light*

### Florida *(1874)*

▲ **The 165-foot (50 m) lighthouse** has a colossal fourth-order Fresnel lens that still remains in operation. Its black and white barber-pole stripes make it a landmark pinnacle of the Florida coast.

▸▸ **Maria de los Dolores Mestre** became the first female lighthouse keeper of St. Augustine after the death of her husband. During the Civil War, Maria removed and hid the lens to deter Union shipping movements.

$\mathcal{S}$t. Augustine Lighthouse is located in the oldest continuing European settlement of North America. As early as 1565, Pedro Menedez, the city's founder, operated a watchtower as a navigational aid at the north end of Anastasia Island, one of the city's barrier islands. In various incarnations the structure was composed first of wood, then coquina (a stone formed of compressed shells) and then brick. The area transferred hands from Spain to Britain, then back to Spain, and finally to the United States in 1821. Paul Pelz, one of the architects of the Library of Congress, designed the lighthouse that remains, which was completed in 1874.

LOCATION: Florida
TOWER HEIGHT: 165 ft. (50 m)
FOCAL PLANE: 161 ft. (49 m)
DAYMARK: Conical structure with black and white spiral bands and a red lantern
LIGHT CHARACTERISTICS: Fixed white light and white flash every 30 seconds
SITE ESTABLISHED: 1823
CURRENT USE: Active

# ● ST. AUGUSTINE *Light*

▸ **The original lighthouse of**
the late 16th century was meant
to aid mariners, but Sir Frances
Drake — on discovering the port
of St. Augustine — pillaged and
destroyed the town and tower.

▸▸ **The beacon served as a Coast**
Guard lookout post for enemy ships
and submarines during World War
II. St. Augustine Light remained
staffed until 1955, when it became
automated.

LOCATION: Michigan
TOWER HEIGHT: 51 ft. (15.5 m)
FOCAL PLANE: 52 ft. (16 m)
DAYMARK: All-red tower
LIGHT CHARACTERISTICS:
Red light every 4 seconds
SITE ESTABLISHED: 1839
CURRENT USE: Active

**The inner light, a conical steel** tower sheathed in cast iron to protect it from fierce winter storms, stands 51 feet (16 m) high from the base of the stone pier. It has a small lantern on top, which originally housed a sixth-order Fresnel lens and today uses a 250-mm optic.

**As boats enter the Grand** Haven River, the Grand Haven Pier Lights guide them into the narrow channel that leads to one of Michigan's best deep-water harbors. The towers, known as the Grand Haven Inner Light and Pier Light, provide what is known by some as the most recognizable of Michigan lights.

*P*ainted fire engine red, the Grand Haven South Pierhead and the Grand Haven South Pier Inner lighthouses sit at opposite ends of a pier that juts out from the shore near the mouth of the Grand Haven River. A small light tower protrudes from the roof of the pierhead light, which is also a fog signal building; this square construction is anchored to a concrete base with a V shape resembling the prow of a ship, which mitigates the effect of waves on the structure. On the other end of a catwalk rises a 51 foot (16 m), steel-sided, cylindrical tower with another light at the top. This unusual pair of twin lights guides boats though one of Lake Michigan's most important harbors.

# GRAND HAVEN

## *Light*
### Michigan *(1839)*

# GRAND HAVEN *Light*

◀◀ **The inner light on the Grand** River, first lit in 1905, is still operational today, under the management of the U.S. Coast Guard. The lantern room, surrounded by a parapet, has been automated since 1969.

▾ **In 1905, the pier was extended** and a catwalk was added to connect the two beacons. The smaller outer tower — which has both a foghorn and a small lantern — was moved to the end of the pier.

# TARRYTOWN

## *Light*

### New York *(1883)*

$\mathcal{I}$n 1847, Congress authorized funds for a lighthouse to warn of dangerous shoals off the eastern shore of the Hudson River, just north of Manhattan. Wrangling over the location delayed construction of the light station, and the completed tower wasn't lit until 1883. The Tappan Zee Bridge spanned the Hudson in 1955 and 6 years later the Tarrytown lighthouse was deactivated. Westchester County took over control of the light in the 1970s and constructed a metal footbridge to connect the lighthouse to the shore. Currently open to the public, the Tarrytown Light celebrated its 125th anniversary in 2008.

**◄◄ Though the light was once a** quarter-mile offshore, retreating waters have brought it a mere 50 feet (15 m) from the mainland.

**► Tarrytown was considered a** desirable lighthouse assignment due to its proximity to town.

LOCATION: New York
TOWER HEIGHT: 60 ft. (18 m)
FOCAL PLANE: None
DAYMARK: White conical spark plug with black gallery and lantern
LIGHT CHARACTERISTICS: None
SITE ESTABLISHED: 1883
CURRENT USE: Inactive

**The keeper's house is actually** inside the lighthouse, the first floor acting as a kitchen and living area, while the bedrooms are on the next two floors. There was a bedroom on the fourth floor as well as a storeroom. The top floor stored equipment for the light.

**The Tarrytown Light is the only** Caisson-style lighthouse on the Hudson River. Caisson lighthouses have cylindrical bases that are sunk into the sea floor then filled with concrete to build the foundation.

**It is called the Tarrytown** Light, but the tower is actually located in Kingsland Point Park in the village of Sleepy Hollow.

# JEFFREY'S HOOK

## *Light*

### New York *(1889)*

▸ **"Once upon a time** a little lighthouse was built on a sharp point of the shore by the Hudson River. It was round and fat and red." This is the opening to the book *The Little Red Lighthouse and the Great Gray Bridge*, which helped save the Jeffrey's Point Light from destruction.

▸▸ **Since 1992, every** September there is a festival held at the lighthouse with readings of Hildegarde Swift's book and other events for children.

▾ **Before the lighthouse** was moved to Fort Washington Park, a red pole with two lanterns on top was the only aid to navigation on Jeffrey's Hook.

𝒯he inspiration for a children's book, Jeffrey's Hook Light, or the Little Red Lighthouse, rests at the edge of the Hudson River. It was built in 1880 at Sandy Hook Point, New Jersey, and was relocated to its current spot in 1921. Ten years later, the George Washington Bridge would tower over the 40-foot (12 m) Jeffrey's Hook Light and make its beacon obsolete. Although plans were afoot for the Coast Guard to auction off the structure, fans of the lighthouse rallied to save it, and in 1951 the Little Red Lighthouse was given to New York City. The light was renovated in 1986, and again in 2000.

LOCATION: New York
TOWER HEIGHT: 40 ft. (12 m)
FOCAL PLANE: 61 ft. (19 m)
DAYMARK: Red tower with
white lantern
LIGHT CHARACTERISTICS:
White light on for 1 second,
off for 2 seconds
SITE ESTABLISHED: 1889
CURRENT USE: Active

LOCATION: Ohio
TOWER HEIGHT: 65 ft. (20 m)
FOCAL PLANE: 67 ft. (20.5 m)
DAYMARK: White tower with red trim
LIGHT CHARACTERISTICS: Green flash every 6 seconds
SITE ESTABLISHED: 1821
CURRENT USE: Active

# MARBLEHEAD
*Light*
Ohio *(1821)*

▲ **As the oldest operational** lighthouse on the Great Lakes, Marblehead Light has been featured on a U.S. postage stamp and on Ohio's license plate.

⊰⊰ **The limestone used to construct** the outer walls and the keeper's house was also used to build the Empire State Building.

Completed in 1821, the Marblehead Lighthouse is the oldest operational lighthouse on the Great Lakes. This gracious structure guides boats to the entrance of Sandusky Bay. The tower was originally 50 feet (15 m) tall, but in 1897 a watch room and a new lighting system were installed to increase the height of the beacon to 65 feet (20 m). A third-order Fresnel lens completed the improvements at that time. Marblehead Light was home to the first female keeper on the Great Lakes, Rachel Wolcott, who took over as keeper after her husband's death. The Wolcott residence is the oldest dwelling in Ottawa County and currently houses a museum where visitors can see the tower's Fresnel lens.

# CHICAGO HARBOR

## *Light*

### Illinois *(1893)*

**▲ The Chicago Harbor**
Light houses a third-order Fresnel lens that was showcased at the World's Fair of 1893. The light wasn't automated until 1979.

**▶ The keeper's quarters**
were built into the 18-foot (5.5 m) diameter tower. This eliminated the expense of and need for a separate building.

The Chicago Harbor Lighthouse is the only surviving lighthouse in Chicago. Originally built at the entrance to the harbor in 1893 in honor of the World's Fair, the light was moved out to the breakwater in 1919. A fog signal building and a boathouse are attached to the light on either side. With red roofs on the buildings and a light characteristic that flashes red every 5 seconds, the Chicago Harbor Light acts not only as an aid to navigation but also as welcome sign to the city.

LOCATION: Illinois
TOWER HEIGHT: 48 ft. (15 m)
FOCAL PLANE: 82 ft. (25 m)
DAYMARK: All-white tower
attached to a building with a
red roof
LIGHT CHARACTERISTICS:
Red flash every 5 seconds
SITE ESTABLISHED: 1832
CURRENT USE: Active

# KILAUEA
## *Light*
### Hawaii *(1913)*

**▲ The ground where** Kilauea Light was built was unstable, and workers had to dig 11 feet (3 m) to find rock solid enough to support the structure. Because of this, Kilauea has a basement.

**◂ In 1927, an army air** crew attempted the first flight from Oakland, California, to Oahu, Hawaii. The crew lost radio signal and were lost until one of the pilots caught sight of the light from Kilauea.

LOCATION: Hawaii
TOWER HEIGHT: 52 ft. (16 m)
FOCAL PLANE: 216 ft. (66 m)
DAYMARK: White tower with red roof on lantern
LIGHT CHARACTERISTICS: None
SITE ESTABLISHED: 1913
CURRENT USE: Active (wildlife refuge)

Located on the north shore of Kauai, Kilauea Lighthouse served as an aid to navigation for ships traveling back and forth from Asia to Hawaii, until the station was damaged in 1976. During its construction the lighthouse at Kilauea met many challenges; all the materials had to be shipped by sea to the island, and when the planned site for the structure was found to be unstable, workers had to dig down 11 feet (3 m) to reach solid rock. As the result of this excavation, the design of the tower was altered to include a basement, an unusual feature in a lighthouse. A second-order Fresnel lens was installed to focus the Kilauea light, and this original lens remains at the station today.

▲ **The lighthouse light was damaged**
while workers tried to automate the light.
A 10-foot (3 m) pole was constructed seaward
of the tower with a rotating beacon in 1976.

▶▶**After the attack on Pearl Harbor**
in 1941, the Kilauea Light was darkened
for the remainder of World War II.

# BARNEGAT

## *Light*

### New Jersey *(1859)*

> **The original optic was a** first-order Fresnel lens. It had 1,027 glass prisms and brass mountings.

> **Though the lighthouse itself** was not deactivated until 1944, a lightship was placed 8 miles (13 km) offshore in 1927, and the Fresnel lens was removed from the lantern room.

Built in 1835, the original Barnegat Light did little to help guide travelers through the waters off the island. George Meade, a government engineer, proclaimed the lighthouse "built of inferior materials" and in 1855 he was commissioned to build a new light. Meade began construction on the beacon the following year, and on January 1, 1859, the new Barnegat Light was lit with a first-order Fresnel lens that shone 165 feet (50 m) above sea level. The beacon was tested by an earthquake later that year, but "Old Barney" was unharmed. Throughout the years the citizens of Barnegat fought to keep the light from disrepair and raised funds to protect the light from erosion. Today, thousands of visitors come to explore the enduring testament to George Meade's vision.

LOCATION: New Jersey
TOWER HEIGHT: 172 ft. (52 m)
FOCAL PLANE: 165 ft. (50 m)
DAYMARK: Top half of tower painted red, lower half painted white
LIGHT CHARACTERISTICS: None
SITE ESTABLISHED: 1859
CURRENT USE: Inactive

# BARNEGAT *Light*

**The wall of Barnegat Light is** almost 5 feet (1.5 m) thick at the base. Two hundred and seventeen stairs lead to the top of the 172-foot (52 m) lighthouse. A 20-room, two-story triplex was constructed to house the three keepers in 1889, but it succumbed to rising waters in 1920.

**Barnegat Inlet was first** discovered by Henry Hudson and was described in an English property deed in 1692.

LOCATION: Mississippi
TOWER HEIGHT: 61 ft. (19 m)
FOCAL PLANE: 48 ft. (15 m)
DAYMARK: All-white tower
with black balustrade
LIGHT CHARACTERISTICS:
White flash every 4 seconds
SITE ESTABLISHED: 1848
CURRENT USE: Active

## Light

### Mississippi *(1848)*

**▲ Shortly after the Civil War,** the Biloxi Light was painted black to protect it from rust. Many believe that this was done as a sign of mourning for the death of Abraham Lincoln. In 1869 the tower was repainted white.

**◄◄ The Biloxi Light is the last** remaining original lighthouse built on the Mississippi coastline.

The Biloxi Light was the first cast iron lighthouse built in the southern United States and the second oldest in the country. Built in 1848 and equipped with a fifth-order Fresnel lens, the light has survived many hurricanes, including the recent onslaught of Katrina — though Hurricane Camille destroyed the keeper's house in 1969. Female keepers have maintained the light at Biloxi longer than at any other lighthouse in the United States. Mary Reynolds was the first female keeper, and she served throughout the Civil War even when the light was darkened. Today the city of Biloxi is being rebuilt after the devastation of Hurricane Katrina, and the lighthouse that weathered the storm is seen as a beacon of hope.

# PORTLAND BREAKWATER

**▲ The Portland Breakwater**
Light has six Corinthian columns
around its perimeter and the roof
edge is decorated with palmettes.
The design was modeled on the
Choragic Monument of Lysicrates
in Athens.

**▸ The original fog bell was**
transported from the Staniford
Ledge buoy every winter to the
breakwater to warn ships of ice. It
was transferred to the breakwater
permanently in 1898.

## *Light*

### Maine *(1875)*

Until 1855 the rubblestone wall of Portland Breakwater remained unlit.
Although it calmed the rough Atlantic waves as they entered the harbor, the
barely discernable breakwater proved a hazard to ships. First an octagonal
wooden beacon shone at the end of the breakwater. Then, when the wall was
lengthened, a temporary lighthouse stood guard. Finally, in 1875, a new tower
modeled on a historic building near Athens replaced the decaying interim
structure. With six cast iron Corinthian columns at its perimeter and Greek
ornamentation on its gallery deck, the lighthouse lit the harbor in style until
1942. The light was reactivated in 2002 as a private aid to navigation.

LOCATION: Maine
TOWER HEIGHT: 26 ft. (8 m)
FOCAL PLANE: 33 ft. (10 m)
DAYMARK: White cast iron
tower with black lantern
LIGHT CHARACTERISTICS:
Fixed red light broken by a
white flash every 40 seconds
SITE ESTABLISHED: 1855
CURRENT USE: Active

# ● PORTLAND BREAKWATER *Light*

▲ **The light's characteristic** changed from a fixed red light to a fixed red light broken by a flash every 40 seconds in 1878.

◄ **The demands of World War II** allowed a shipbuilding company to take over the land surrounding the breakwater. The light was deactivated in 1942.

# UP THE SPIRAL STAIRCASE

**Accessing the lantern room** atop a tall tower is like any worthwhile but daunting enterprise, a formidable task, taken one step at a time. Each lighthouse has its own version of a path to the top, but the spiral has been most commonly adopted because it is efficient both in terms of function and space. Materials such as wood, stone, brick and cast iron have been used as the building blocks of the ascent. A walk up the stairs of a lighthouse puts visitors in close contact with the challenges of times long past.

Many of the builders of early American lighthouses used wooden planks for stairs because lumber was readily available and easy to work with. As the timbers aged and rotted they often became soaked with the fuel, be it whale oil, lard or kerosene, that was regularly hauled upward. The result was that many lighthouses ended their service by going up in flames.

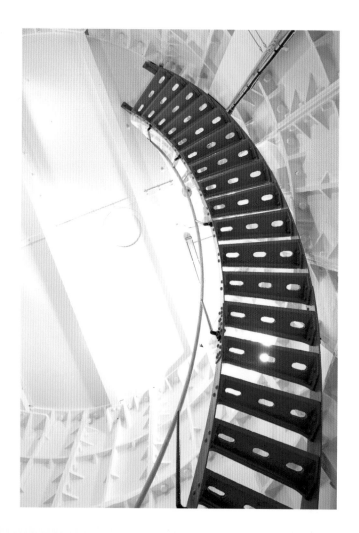

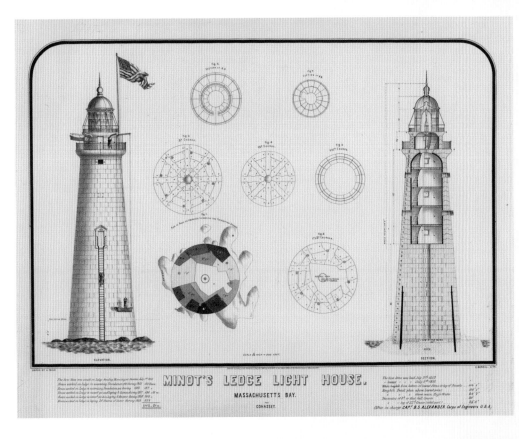

MINOT'S LEDGE LIGHT HOUSE.
MASSACHUSETTS BAY.
COHASSET.

◁ **This lithograph of Minot's** Ledge Light in Massachusetts was made in 1860. It is a measured drawing including elevation and breaks the light down into sections.

◁◁ **Cast iron staircases have** replaced earlier wood, stone and brick models because of their resilience to fire, varying weights and aging.

◢ **The Ponce de Leon Light** is Florida's tallest lighthouse. It takes 194 steps with nine landings to reach the lantern room.

▾ **Built in the Cape Cod** style, the Old Point Loma Light in California has a central spiral staircase leading to the lantern room.

Stone and brick proved to be sturdier and longer lasting. Even when the British set fire to Jamestown, Rhode Island's, Beavertail Light (1856), the revolutionaries were able to repair the stone tower and stairs instead of counting them a total loss. Cast iron was the next innovation. These staircases were made to order, at forges in San Francisco and elsewhere, and then delivered to the site. Cast iron stairs stood up well to the rigors of lighthouse life.

Early keepers commonly dragged great loads of fuel to the top of the long flight. Eighty-pound (36 kg) drums of whale oil were heaved upward every day in the 1700s. The keeper also ascended the tower each night to tend the light, polish the lantern and wind the works. Some died or were injured in falls on the steep stairs. Rotten or cracked or rusty, weak or sound, these steps were the foundation of the crucial work of the lighthouse keepers.

# LOST LIGHTHOUSES

Wars, heavy weather, obsolescence, erosion and neglect all have toppled their share of lighthouses. Many historic and picturesque lights now exist only in photographs, written records and the memories of a few ancients. The stories of these lights, heroes of days gone by, give us a glimpse of the birth of lighthouse history in North America.

The original Boston Light, completed on Little Brewster Island in 1716, was the first lighthouse to grace the shores of the colonies that would become the United States. This tower, said to be of nearly the same dimensions as its successor, faced many battles in its 60 years. It was gutted by unintentional fire in 1751 and struck by lightning several times. Religious locals delayed the installment of a lightning rod because they thought it "vanity and irreligion" to tamper with the will of God. Eventually, common sense prevailed, and a lightning conductor was set in place. This light was also home to the first fog signal, a cannon, suggested by keeper John Hayes.

The British seized the Boston Light in 1775, and less than a month later American troops lit a fire in the tower. The light was repaired, and again the colonial forces invaded and set the tower ablaze. Finally in 1776, as the vanquished British were fleeing for their

**▲ Cleveland Harbor East Pierhead gazes** out over Lake Erie and her west-pier sister light. In its early days the East Pierhead Light was the site of many courageous rescue efforts, including that of the assistant keeper who saved the crew of the *John T. Johnson*, a schooner-rigged barge.

**◄◄ A 1780 etching of Cape Henlopen** reveals the sandy shoreline that eventually caused the octagonal stone tower to collapse. Previous to its demolition in 1926, the lighthouse had been subject to a grueling fire set by British troops during the Revolutionary War.

**▸ The original 70-foot (21 m) tall** structure was built with the theory that waves would harmlessly pass through its spidery legs. Yet, many of its keepers quit after calling the light "unsafe." In 1851 a storm swept away Minot's Ledge.

lives, the soldiers lit a long fuse, setting off a timed explosion that reduced the strategic asset to rubble.

As deadly as dynamite, mighty ocean surges proved invincible antagonists to offshore light stations, such as the skeletal tower at Minot's Ledge. The experimental light, built in 1850, succumbed to the huge waves of a gale a year later. The two assistant keepers on duty at the time lost their lives but kept the bell ringing and the fire lit until a breaker swept the tower off its steel legs. A lighthouse's battle with destiny is not always a dramatic tussle. Some lights, such as Cape Henlopen in Delaware, survived revolution only to later fall to erosion. The Cleveland Lighthouse, with its Byzantine tower and High-Victorian keepers' quarters, lit the Cleveland Harbor in elegant style for close to two decades. This ornate edifice was supplanted in the early 1890s by a simple breakwater light. The elaborate, outmoded station was eventually dismantled. Although lost, the valor and beauty of these lights live on in the imagination.

**◄ Built in 1860 and designed** by General Joseph G. Totten, the new Minot's Light survived countless nor'easters because its 3,514 tons of granite and iron provided sturdy support against 170-foot (52 m) waves.

**◄◄ Minot's Light was last seen** violently swaying 2 feet (61 cm) in either direction at 10 o'clock the night of the tempest. At daylight, the horizon was vacant, but Minot's bell could be heard clanking as it drifted ashore.

**◄ During the Colonial era Boston** Harbor Light oversaw the commercial hub of maritime traffic and trade. When the British finally set fire to the lighthouse on June 13, 1776, colonial troops salvaged the remains of the beacon's metal lantern to use for their cannons.

**▼ Erected in 1870, the Cleveland** Lighthouse sits on the west pier of the harbor, marking the Cuyahoga River entrance. Unfortunately, the Victorian Gothic Lighthouse was severely damaged in a fire and was put out of service around 1900.

# *Square* CONSTRUCTION

SQUARE LIGHTHOUSE construction draws on the assumptions of typical residential architecture, and some, such as the Hereford Inlet Light in New Jersey, incorporate Victorian elements. The square model is the least common style of lighthouse tower in North America. Although both are four-sided, square towers have a constant diameter from top to bottom, and square pyramidal towers taper from a wide base to a narrower top. In the case of Eagle Bluff Light in Wisconsin, a square tower was chosen so that the daymark would be easily distinguishable from other lights on the coast. They are less streamlined than their conical, cylindrical, hexagonal or octagonal counterparts, but some square towers, such as Race Rocks Light in British Columbia, were built to last. This granite beauty, made from stone hewn in Scotland, has watched over Victoria Harbour since the mid-1900s.

◀ **Presque Isle North Pierhead Lighthouse,** Pennsylvania

LOCATION: California
TOWER HEIGHT: 48 ft. (15 m)
FOCAL PLANE: 273 ft. (83 m)
DAYMARK: Square concrete tower, cylindrical black lantern and gallery, red lantern roof
LIGHT CHARACTERISTICS: White flash every 15 seconds
SITE ESTABLISHED: 1889
CURRENT USE: Active

▶▶**The first-order Fresnel lens** from Point Sur Light can be found on display at the Maritime Museum of Monterey. In 2001, the lighthouse lantern room underwent a complete restoration.

▼ **It took 11 years of petitioning** for Congress to allocate the funds to build a lighthouse on Point Sur. In 1975 the captain of the *Ventura* crashed on the rocks of Point Sur while intoxicated; many passengers died.

# *Light*

## California *(1889)*

In 1874, the Lighthouse Board recommended a new light to close the gap on the Californian coast between Piedras Blancas and Pigeon Point. Permission was not granted until 1889, after numerous requests and several shipwrecks near the point caused concern. Stones for the tower were quarried from the surrounding hills, and the structure was anchored to the 361-foot (110 m) tall rock. The actual tower is located in a depression in the rock so that it is visible below the fog line. The current light station has been beautifully restored and includes many of the original support buildings, as well as the barn, the blacksmith/carpenter shop and the water tower.

# WEST POINT

## *Light*

### Prince Edward Island *(1876)*

The square, tapered tower at West Point was one of the first lighthouses built on Prince Edward Island. First lit in 1876, the tower was originally painted red and white, but in 1915 it was changed to black and white. The new color scheme was thought to be more noticeable from sea. A keeper's house was attached to the tower, but part of the living space, including bedrooms, were actually located within the tower itself. Today the light acts as an inn, with a restaurant next door. Visitors can stay in the tower bedrooms.

▸▸**West Point had only two keepers in the 87 years of** operation before automation. William MacDonald served as keeper until 1925 and Benjamin MacIsaac until 1963.

▾**The square structure of the tower became popular in** the late 1860s after Canada became an independent nation.

LOCATION:
Prince Edward Island
**TOWER HEIGHT:** 66 ft. (20 m)
**FOCAL PLANE:** 67 ft. (20 m)
**DAYMARK:** Square tower with
black and white stripes
**LIGHT CHARACTERISTICS:**
White light — 6 seconds on,
6 seconds off
**SITE ESTABLISHED:** 1876
**CURRENT USE:** Active

LOCATION: Pennsylvania
TOWER HEIGHT: 67 ft. (20 m)
FOCAL PLANE: 73 ft. (22 m)
DAYMARK: White square tower
with black lantern
LIGHT CHARACTERISTICS:
White flash — 3 seconds on
and 3 seconds off
SITE ESTABLISHED: 1872
CURRENT USE: Active

▲ **There are 76 steps from the base** to the top of the tower. The lantern room housed a fourth-order Fresnel lens.

◄◄ **The "Sidewalk Trail" that connected** the light to the boathouse on Misery Bay was paved in 1925 and can still be walked today.

ocated on the north shore of the Presque Isle Peninsula off Lake Erie, the Presque Isle Light has assisted ships navigating these waters for more than 100 years. First lit in 1873, the 40-foot (12 m) light is built into the keeper's house. It was inaccessible by land until a 1.5-mile (2.5 km) pathway was constructed. For more than 20 years, the tower went unpainted, with the original daymark of natural brick blending in with the house. In 1899 the tower was painted white to create a more prominent daymark for ships. Modernization has changed the external structure very little, though the light is now fully automated and some additions have been added to the keeper's house.

# PRESQUE ISLE NORTH PIERHEAD

*Light*

**Pennsylvania** *(1858)*

𝒯he Presque Island North Pierhead Light marks the mouth of the Presque Isle Bay. Built in 1858 to replace a former beacon that had been destroyed by a ship, the light has been moved twice: in 1882 and 1940 to accommodate the changing pier. In 1940 the structure was reinforced with steel plates. The light housed a fourth-order Fresnel lens until 1995, when a solar-powered optic was installed. The Coast Guard now uses the keeper's house, a short distance from the light.

**◄◄ Though the tower is closed to** the public, visitors can walk the pier to the light and watch boats sail by in the lake.

**▶ Presque Isle is French for** "almost an island," which is fitting because Presque Isle is a peninsula.

LOCATION: Pennsylvania
TOWER HEIGHT: 34 ft. (10 m)
FOCAL PLANE: 42 ft. (13 m)
DAYMARK: White square tower with black band and black gallery
LIGHT CHARACTERISTICS: Red flash every 2.5 seconds
SITE ESTABLISHED: 1858
CURRENT USE: Active

LOCATION: Rhode Island
TOWER HEIGHT: 45 ft. (14 m)
FOCAL PLANE: 68 ft. (21 m)
DAYMARK: Square white tower,
with a lantern and gallery
LIGHT CHARACTERISTICS:
White flash every 6 seconds
SITE ESTABLISHED: 1749
CURRENT USE: Active

## *Light*

### Rhode Island *(1856)*

Rhode Island rum was quite popular in Europe and elsewhere in the early 18th century, and the active trading of slaves, rum and molasses between Jamestown, West Africa, and the Caribbean Islands made for a busy harbor at Newport. In 1749 the first lighthouse was established on the southern tip of Coanicut Island, known as Beavertail Point. It was the third lighthouse in what would become the United States. This structure was destroyed in a fire, and its successor survived until 1856, when the aging edifice was replaced. The square, granite tower erected on the site withstood the fury of the hurricane of 1938, although the whistle house was swept away. Many early fog signal instruments were tested here, including the Daboll trumpet.

**Vandals once shot out the Beavertail** Light in 1975, and for several days ships were unable to see its guiding light.
**Beavertail Light had a woman keeper** for nine years when Demaris H. Weeden took over for her husband, Robert, after his death in 1848.

# HORTON POINT

## Light

### New York *(1857)*

The Horton Point Lighthouse began as a gleam in George Washington's eye as he rode his horse across Long Island on the way to Boston in 1756. He discussed the suitability of the site with Ezra L'Hommedieu at that time, but his vision would not come to fruition until more than 100 years later. The Scottish immigrant William Sinclair supervised the construction of the granite, brick and wood light station, which was completed in 1857. In 1871 a new layer of mortar was applied to shore up the brickwork. After its duties were transferred to a nearby 40-foot (12 m) skeletal tower in 1933, the lighthouse was neglected for decades. On the brink of being demolished in the 1970s, the building was saved and restored by the Southhold Historical Society.

▲ **Horton Point Light has had only eight keepers** throughout its history, including one woman — Stella Price — who served for 2 months while the keeper was recovering from injury.

▸▸ **Horton Point Light was inactive** for more than half a century until it was relit in June 1990 and returned to active service.

LOCATION: New York
TOWER HEIGHT: 58 ft. (18 m)
FOCAL PLANE: 103 ft. (31 m)
DAYMARK: Square white
granite tower, black lantern
and gallery
LIGHT CHARACTERISTICS:
Green flash every 10 seconds
SITE ESTABLISHED: 1857
CURRENT USE: Active

LOCATION: Michigan
TOWER HEIGHT: 45 ft. (14 m)
FOCAL PLANE: 52 ft. (16 m)
DAYMARK: Square red tower, lantern and gallery
LIGHT CHARACTERISTICS: Flashes every 10 seconds, alternating red and white
SITE ESTABLISHED: 1872
CURRENT USE: Active

# HOLLAND HARBOR

*Light*

Michigan *(1872)*

▲ **The steamboat *Huron* was the first ship to pass** through the newly crafted canal Reverend A.C. Van Raalte had built between Black Lake and Lake Michigan.

◀ **After complaints from captains that fog was** obstructing the view of the light, the U.S. Congress funded the erection of a fog signal building in 1907.

$\mathcal{W}$hen a request to Congress for an allocation to clear sandbars and silt for a channel didn't result in sufficient funds for the job, a hearty colony of Dutch settlers from Holland, Michigan, took matters into their own hands. They dug a channel from Lake Macatawa, also known as Black Lake, to Lake Michigan. The effort was completed on July 1, 1859, when the small steamboat *Huron* slipped through the newly deepened waterway. Increased shipping traffic resulted, and a pierhead beacon was built in 1872 to light the entrance to the drowned river mouth. Improvements, such as lengthening the pier and replacing wood with cast iron, has increased the efficacy and longevity of the station. The 1907 fog signal building and the 1936 tower that rises from its west end currently stand guard over the waterway, and the two together are affectionately called "Big Red" by locals.

**▲ The Holland Harbor Light was** nicknamed "Big Red" after being painted red in the 1950s. It received the new coat of paint because a dictum instructed that lighthouses on the right side of the entrance to a harbor must be red.

**◄◄ In the 1960s the fourth-order** Frensel lens was removed from the light and replaced with a 250-mm Tidelands Signal acrylic optic.

**▶ Big Red was saved from** destruction by concerned citizens, who fought for the preservation of the lighthouse in the 1970s. The Holland Harbor Lighthouse Historical Commission was created to care for the lighthouse, and in 2007 the light was officially transferred to the Commission.

LOCATION: British Columbia
TOWER HEIGHT: 35 ft. (11 m)
FOCAL PLANE: 41 ft. (12 m)
DAYMARK: Square red tower,
lantern and gallery
LIGHT CHARACTERISTICS:
Brief white flashes
SITE ESTABLISHED: 1890
CURRENT USE: Active

*Light*

## Bristish Columbia *(1915)*

Brockton Point was named for British engineer Francis Brockton, who found a vein of coal in Vancouver in 1859. An aid to vessels navigating the Burrard Inlet, the lighthouse sits on the 5.5-mile (9 km) long seawall that encircles Stanley Park. Every year the picturesque setting attracts millions of visitors who walk, bike and skate on the long path around the park. The nine o'clock gun, originally a signal from the lighthouse keeper that fishing was closed, is still fired off electronically every night.

▲ **Brockton Point is located above the seawall, so that** promenaders can walk right under it.

◀ **The tower that stands today on Brockton Point** is not the first. The original was built in 1890.

# ILLUMINATION

▾ **In 1822 the first Fresnel lens was** lit at France's Corduan lighthouse that stands at the mouth of the Gironde estuary. Its beacon was visible up to 20 nautical miles out at sea. Soon after, the Fresnel lens was shipped to the United States and became a staple in stations guarding both coasts.

The desire to send an illuminating ray of light into the night sky has awakened the ingenuity of problem solvers and inventors for millennia. From bonfires on high hills to single candles whose diffused light is focused by multiprismed, three-ton lenses, to automated aerobeacons powered by electronic impulses, the technology associated with the guiding beam of the lighthouse has evolved over time.

The wood and coal fires of early lighthouses consumed huge amounts of fuel and exacted grueling hours of toil from their keepers. Simple bonfires were probably the first tools used to warn ships of rocky coastlines or shoals. The Pharos Colossus at Alexandria is one of the oldest known lighthouses that used an open fire. The towers at Falsterbo in Sweden (1793) and North Foreland (1691) and Lizard Point (1751) in England are examples of lighthouses that utilized coal to fuel their beacons. Coal fires were lit in a chauffer or brazier, which allowed the light to gleam from the container.

These early techniques for throwing light were made obsolete by wick-and-oil technology. In 1780 Aimé Argand invented a hollow wicked lamp that burned six to eight times as brightly as a single candle. Vaporized paraffin, whale and colza (rapeseed) oil, lard, acetylene

AUGUSTIN JEAN FRESNEL
(Physicien),
Membre de l'Académie des Sciences.
Né à Broglie (Dépt de l'Eure) le 10 Mai 1788.

▲ **Fresnel lenses are divided into seven orders** depending on the distance of the flame to the lens. A first-order Fresnel lens is 7 feet, 10 inches (239 cm) in height while a fourth-order lens would only be 2 feet, 4 inches (71 cm).

▼ **In 1822 the French physician Augustin-Jean** Fresnel engineered and developed the first Fresnel lens. Due to his studies of optic light wave theory he was able to discover that surface curvature gave the lens its focusing power.

◀ **This drawing of the landscape of the lantern** room in the Cape Hatteras Light in North Carolina is broken into sections and shows how the lantern room will be accessible.

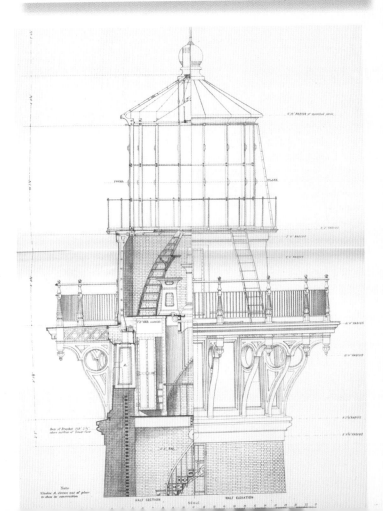

and kerosene serviced the lamps of some of the New World's lighthouses. A silvered brass bowl harnessed a portion of the light that had previously been lost in dispersion and reflected it back out to sea. Most sources credit this tool to Argand, but Winslow Lewis' version of the parabolic reflector was used in the young American colonies. In 1882 the Fresnel lens — which had been popular in Europe for decades — proved itself far superior.

Sailors blasted Stephen Pleasonton, the fifth auditor of the U.S. treasury, for equipping lighthouses with Lewis's reflectors, even though the innovative Fresnel lens could cast a beam that reached 5 and sometimes 10 miles (16 km) farther. When the Fresnel lens was finally taken up in America, the intricate system of prisms would grace the lanterns of nearly every lighthouse along its coasts.

# ANATOMY OF THE *Fresnel Lens*

▸ **The cutaway drawing of a lighthouse** lantern room from the mid-1800s depicts a Fresnel lens that was exhibited at the Paris Universal Exposition of 1855. Standing 10 feet (3 m) tall, the cylindrical lens has a clockwork mechanism (M) and a pendulum-like weight (P) that rotates the lens on six rollers (A, B).

**The earliest Fresnel lens consisted of a** lamp made of 5 wicks fueled by whale oil and kerosene. Incandescent lamps replaced the oil, and the rays of the new lamp created an illuminating beam of 80,000 candle power.

▾ **Each Fresnel lens, such as the Loschen** lighthouse's lens in Bremerhaven, Germany, is composed of concentric rings of glass prisms that bend light into narrow beams. At the center of the lens is the bull's-eye, which functions similarly to a magnifying glass, intensifying the refracted light. Each lens section is bound together by brass frames that increase the weight of the entire lens to as much as 8 tons.

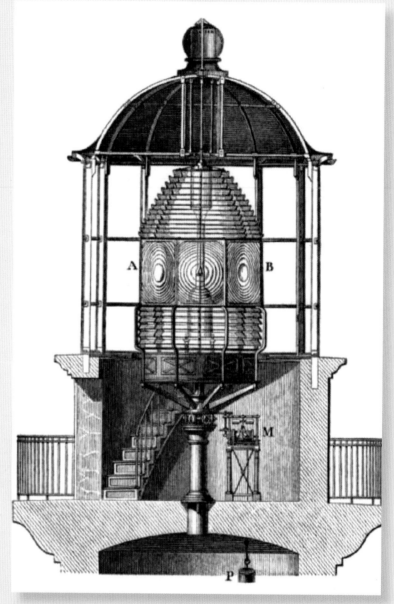

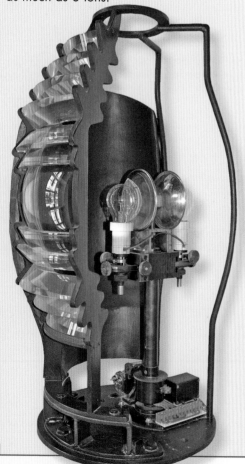

A Fresnel lens resembles a crystal beehive. The lens surrounds the lamp with hundreds of individual pieces of ground glass that refract and reflect approximately 80 percent of the source's light and concentrate it into a powerful beam. Reaching as far as 25 miles (40 km), the light source of the Fresnel lens was usually raised approximately 100 feet (30 m) above sea level, making it visible above the curvature of the earth.

Aerobeacons positioned on skeletal towers or large buoys are the modern choice for navigational illumination. These efficient lamps are often solar powered and have replaced many Fresnels in recent years. Repairing a damaged Fresnel lens can be a costly, time-consuming endeavor; standardized parts for an aerobeacon are readily available. Still, many appreciate the beauty and efficacy of the Fresnel lens and recognize its great contribution to the lives of generations of seafaring people. Historical societies across America are restoring and preserving these lenses as reminders of our past and a celebration of the golden years of lighthouses.

▲ **A key design point of the Fresnel lens is its** modular construction, as the lens can be built in one location, disassembled, shipped and reassembled in the limited space of the lantern.

◄ **Erected in 1895 Oregon's Cape Meares Lighthouse** has a first-order Fresnel lens with eight sides, four primary lenses and four bull's-eye lenses. The light alternates between flashes red and white that can be seen by vessels up to 21 miles (34 km) at sea.

# Hexagonal & Octagonal
## CONSTRUCTION

**HEXAGONAL AND OCTAGONAL** towers have walls that radiate symmetrically from a center point. This balanced and efficient architectural style creates a nondirectional stability that is very successful in surviving high-impact threats, such as earthquakes, strong winds and powerful waves. Bends or folds in the tower's footprint reinforce the connection to the foundation, granting the structure additional strength. Many screw-pile lighthouses utilize this geometry because screw-pile legs easily support six- or eight-sided constructions. Historic beacons, such as the tower at Sandy Hook, New Jersey, the oldest operating light in the country, demonstrate the resilience and longevity of lighthouses built on this model.

◀ **St. Ignace Lighthouse,**
Michigan

# TYBEE ISLAND

## Light
### Georgia (1773)

The original station at Tybee Island was built in 1736, under the watchful eye of James Oglethorpe, founder of the colony of Georgia. The first light on the island, a 90-foot (27 m) tower, was destroyed in a fierce storm. Five years later, the encroaching sea undermined a second tower. The third tower, a brick edifice with wooden landings and stairs, was erected in 1773. It was elevated to the height of 150 feet (46 m) in 1867, and this last incarnation currently stands guard at Tybee. The tower and support buildings have been beautifully restored, making this light one of the most historically intact stations in the United States.

▸▸**Confederate troops set fire to the light during the Civil War in order to** prevent Union troops from using it. The troops also built an army barracks which was later used as a keeper's house.

▾ **After the Civil War, the Tybee light was rebuilt from the then-existing** structure, and a first-order Fresnel lens was placed in the lantern.

LOCATION: Georgia
TOWER HEIGHT: 145 ft. (44 m)
FOCAL PLANE: 144 ft. (44 m)
DAYMARK: Painted black with
a white band
LIGHT CHARACTERISTICS:
Fixed white light
SITE ESTABLISHED: 1736
CURRENT USE: Active

◄ **The lighthouse that stands on Tybee Island today,** made of masonry and metal only, is completely fireproof.

◄◄ **The daymark of the Tybee Island Light has** changed over time, though its current mark was originally on the light from 1916 to 1965. The light has had six different daymarks throughout its history.

▲ **In 2003 the Tybee Island Light was featured on** a commemorative U.S. postage stamp.

# CAPE ARAGO

## *Light*
### Oregon *(1934)*

$\mathcal{I}$n 2008 the confederated tribes of the Coos, Lower Umpqua and Siuslaw Indians took possession of the recently deactivated lighthouse at Cape Arago. The light is located on a detached spit of land, known as Chief Island, that has served native tribes as a burial ground for generations. The third lighthouse erected on the island and the high bridge to the mainland are the only structures that remain. The present-day tower, built of reinforced concrete in 1934, makes this edifice one of the youngest beacons on the Oregon coast.

▲ **The Cape Arago Light was originally built in 1866, 10 years** after the first white settlers arrived on Chief Island.

▸ **After several attempts at building a low bridge to the island** failed, a pulley system was installed in 1891. Seven years later, tragedy struck when one of the cages fell from the pulley, injuring the lightkeeper and his family.

LOCATION: Oregon
TOWER HEIGHT: 44 ft. (13 m)
FOCAL PLANE: 100 ft. (30 m)
DAYMARK: White tower with green lantern and red dome
LIGHT CHARACTERISTICS: None
SITE ESTABLISHED: 1866
CURRENT USE: Inactive

◀◀ **In 1909, a third lighthouse was** built on Cape Arago after erosion endangered the old lighthouse and the fog signal building.

▶ **The Cape Arago light was** deactivated in 2006, though many are interested in keeping the light active and opening it to the public.

▼ **The Indian tribes of the area** obtained an Indian Burial Ground Easement just opposite the light in 1975. The Coos Indians had a strong connection to Chief Island — many of their ancestors were buried there.

# ALCATRAZ ISLAND

## *Light*
### California *(1909)*

*B*efore the prison, before the riots, before Al Capone, "the Rock" was known as La Isla de los Alcatraces, the Island of the Pelicans. The U.S. government commissioned Francis Gibbons to build a lighthouse on the island because it was directly in line with the Golden Gate and could guide vessels through the strait into San Francisco Bay. The short tower of the Cape Cod–style lighthouse rose from the center of the keeper's quarters, and its light provided guidance to the booming maritime traffic of the gold rush. Later demolished to build a military fortification, and then a federal prison, the original Alcatraz Island Light was the first lighthouse on the Pacific coast. Its successor, an 84-foot (26 m) concrete tower, stands next to the now-abandoned cells of the infamous penitentiary.

▸▸ **The original Alcatraz Light** was the first lighthouse on the Pacific Coast. It was lit in 1854, years prior to the island becoming a prison locale.

▸ **When the prison was built** in 1909, the original lighthouse was torn down, and the current concrete tower was built with a fourth-order Fresnel lens.

LOCATION: California
TOWER HEIGHT: 84 ft. (26 m)
FOCAL PLANE: 214 ft. (65 m)
DAYMARK: Octagonal
unpainted concrete with black
trim on gallery
LIGHT CHARACTERISTICS:
White flash every 5 seconds
SITE ESTABLISHED: 1854
CURRENT USE: Active

ALCATRAZ LIGHTHOUSE, SAN FRANCISCO BAY: FIRST LIGHT ON THE PACIFIC COAST

From a drawing by Major Hartman Bache, 1859

**Alcatraz takes its name** from the Spanish word *alcatraces*. Popular belief is that the word means "pelican," but the literal translation is "gannet," the name of another seabird of the rocky coasts.

**An earthquake in 1906** destroyed the warden's house, the keepers' quarters, and several other buildings on the island. The light is the only remaining building.

**From 1935 to the present, 11** movies have been filmed about and on this island off the San Francisco coast.

# MONTAUK POINT

## *Light*

### New York *(1796)*

$\mathcal{M}$ontauk Point Light is located at the tip of Long Island on a tortoise-shaped mound known as Turtle Hill. President George Washington and the Second Congress authorized construction on that sight in 1792. The first glimpse of America for many immigrants, Montauk Point Light has served as a beacon of hope for sailors and passengers alike. Strong walls, 7 feet (2 m) thick at the base, and a deep foundation have fortified this monument against the ravages of storms. When the encroaching sea threatened the foundation, New Yorker Georgina Reid suggested digging trenches on the eroding hill and stuffing them with grass to help stop erosion and encourage the growth of other plants. This simple, yet innovative method has proven quite effective, and the country's fourth-oldest light is temporarily safe, although other long-term solutions are still under consideration.

▲ **Located on the tip of Long Island, Montauk Point** Light is the oldest lighthouse in New York State, completed in 1796.

▶▶ **Montauk Point Light is whitewashed and its** brown band repainted every year to ensure the station's upkeep and visibility.

LOCATION: New York
TOWER HEIGHT: 110 ft. (34 m)
FOCAL PLANE: 168 ft. (51 m)
DAYMARK: Octagonal white
tower with a single wide
brown band and black lantern
LIGHT CHARACTERISTICS:
White flash every 5 seconds
SITE ESTABLISHED: 1796
CURRENT USE: Active

**◄◄ In 1987, the Keepers' House** was turned into a museum, where the second-order Fresnel lens from the lantern room can be found. The current tower is lit with a modern light that can be seen for 19 nautical miles (35 km).

**▸ During the Revolutionary War,** the British invasion of New York through Montauk Point led to the building of a coastal observation deck and a submarine-spotting tower. Both buildings and several gun emplacements still remain.

**▾ Since the American Revolution,** Montauk Point's biggest enemy is the erosion of the land around its base.

# MONTAUK POINT *Light*

▲ **A feature story in the September 1871 edition of *Harper's*** magazine described a visit to the lighthouse. The writer enjoyed "the comfortable fireside of the keeper's family." There he sat with the family, "listening to stories of storms from the southeast."

▶ **The light burned whale oil for 50 years, until whales** became scarce. Lard oil then was substituted until kerosene replaced it as a fuel in the 1860s.

LOCATION: Nova Scotia
TOWER HEIGHT: 43 ft. (13 m)
FOCAL PLANE: 72 ft. (22 m)
DAYMARK: Octagonal
structure with concrete tower
and lantern painted white with
red trim
LIGHT CHARACTERISTICS:
Fixed green light
SITE ESTABLISHED: 1868
CURRENT USE: Active

▲ **The original light was built** in 1868. It was a wooden house with a beacon on the roof.

▶▶ **Peggy's Point Light has had** many different colored lights. Its original was a red light, its next was white and its current light, installed in 1979, shines green.

# PEGGY'S POINT

## *Light*

### Nova Scotia *(1914)*

℘he town bordering on St. Margaret's Bay became known as Peggy's Cove, perhaps as an affectionate nickname for the bay or, as the region's tales suggest, because of an inspiring shipwrecked girl who swam her way to safety on the coast many years earlier. In any case, the sturdy octagonal tower built there in 1914 and the lively local folklore of the surrounding community attract throngs of visitors following the scenic Lighthouse Route that runs along the south shore of Nova Scotia from Halifax to Yarmouth. Other notable beacons on this trail are the lights at Fort Point (Liverpool) and Seal Island.

# PEGGY'S POINT *Light*

▸ **The lower level of the light has been** made into a post office, where visitors can send postcards directly from the light.

▸▸ **The current tower was built in 1914,** only 50 feet (15 m) west of the original light. It is made of concrete.

▾ **In 1969 the lantern tower was** painted red. It was originally white.

# PEGGY'S POINT *Light*

◀ **Despite warnings of the** dangerous, unpredictable currents around Peggy's Cove, several tourists drown off the coast each season.

▶▶ **Peggy's Point Light is one of** the most visited and photographed lighthouses in the world.

▼ **Peggy's Cove is a tiny fishing** village that can claim only about 50 year-round residents.

▸▸**The Sandy Hook Light is**
105 feet (32 m) tall and its base
has a 29-foot (9 m) diameter. At
its base the walls are 7 feet (2 m)
thick.

▾ **The light has been darkened**
only twice in its long history,
during the American Revolution
and World War II.

LOCATION: New Jersey
TOWER HEIGHT: 85 ft. (26 m)
FOCAL PLANE: 88 ft. (27 m)
DAYMARK: Octagonal white
tower with red lantern
LIGHT CHARACTERISTICS:
Fixed white light
SITE ESTABLISHED: 1764
CURRENT USE: Active

# SANDY HOOK

## *Light*

**New Jersey** *(1764)*

$\mathcal{T}$he oldest functioning lighthouse in the United States, the beacon at Sandy Hook has marked the entrance of New York Harbor since 1764. Money for the project was raised by lottery, and Isaac Conro oversaw the construction of the octagonal, rubble-stone tower. Early in the Revolutionary War the British occupied the tower. Daring rebel artillery soldiers sought to destroy this strategic asset to no avail; the cannonballs the men fired just bounced off the sturdy sentinel. Instead of being endangered by erosion, Sandy Hook Light is experiencing littoral drift. The structure, originally 500 feet (152 m) from the ocean, now resides almost 1.5 miles (2.5 km) from the shoreline.

# SANDY HOOK *Light*

▲ **Sandy Hook was the first light in the** country to go electric, when in 1889 it was equipped with incandescent lamps.

◄ **Automated in 1962, Sandy Hook** Lighthouse still has a third-order Fresnel lens that can be seen 19 miles (31 km) out at sea.

▶▶**Though located in New Jersey,** Sandy Hook was funded by a New York State lottery. The original lighthouse was restored in 2000.

LOCATION: California
TOWER HEIGHT: 47 ft. (14 m)
FOCAL PLANE: 84 ft. (26 m)
DAYMARK: Octagonal tower
with brown trim, black lantern
and gallery
LIGHT CHARACTERISTICS:
White flash every 10 seconds
SITE ESTABLISHED: 1909
CURRENT USE: Active

*Light*

California *(1909)*

**The third-order Fresnel lens in** the lantern room of the light is one of only three British-built lenses in operation in the United States.

**Though a light wasn't built until** 1909, the U.S. Lighthouse Service had surveyed Point Cabrillo in 1873.

*S*ailors called the agile vessels that could navigate the narrow passages and ports along the California coast "doghole schooners," because they squeezed like nimble dogs through the tight waterways. Traffic from these and other vessels increased as San Francisco sought lumber from the Mendocino sawmills to rebuild after the great earthquake of 1906. That same year, Congress approved $50,000 for a light at Point Cabrillo. The lighthouse, completed in 1909, resembles a church; its octagonal tower rises from a one-and-a-half-story fog signal station. Many of the original support buildings have been restored, including the blacksmith shop, oil house and the keeper's dwelling, which now serves as a museum.

POINT CABRILLO LIGHT • 201

# GIBRALTAR POINT

## *Light*

### Ontario *(1808)*

$\mathcal{G}$ibraltar Point Light hovers over the Toronto harbor of Lake Ontario. A beautiful 52-foot (16 m) tall stone tower was erected in 1808 and then raised to 82 feet (25 m) in 1832. The original exterior structure is intact, and much of the interior architecture — including the Douglas fir stairs that spiral to the lantern — has been in place since 1870. Stories of the first keeper, a friendly, beer-brewing fellow, and his heinous murder on a blustery night keep visitors coming. Some have claimed to have heard the sound of something large and heavy being dragged up the tower stairs.

LOCATION: Ontario
TOWER HEIGHT: 82 ft. (25 m)
FOCAL PLANE: None
DAYMARK: Hexagonal tower with red lantern and gallery
LIGHT CHARACTERISTICS: Fixed green light (decorative)
SITE ESTABLISHED: 1808
CURRENT USE: Inactive

▸ **The Gibraltar Point light is the** second-oldest lighthouse in Canada and the oldest light in Ontario.

◂◂ **Electricity was introduced to** Gibraltar Point in 1916, and the light pattern was changed to a white light blinking on and off. In 1945 the light color was changed to green.

▶▶ **Both of the Cape Henry** lighthouses had delays in construction. The American Revolution delayed Old Cape Henry by 18 years, and the New Cape Henry Light experienced a series of construction mishaps before it was completed in 1881.

◀ **The Old Cape Henry Light** was the first federal construction project under the Constitution.

▼ **The unique Cape Henry** Light daymark is often likened to a checkerboard because of its alternating black and white color scheme.

LOCATION: Virginia
TOWER HEIGHT: 164 ft. (50 m)
FOCAL PLANE: 164 ft. (50 m)
DAYMARK: Octagonal tower with black and white vertical alternating stripes and a black lantern
LIGHT CHARACTERISTICS: 3 flashes every 20 seconds
SITE ESTABLISHED: 1792
CURRENT USE: Active

# CAPE HENRY

*Light*

**Virginia** *(1881)*

*O*n its first session in 1789, the U.S. Congress commissioned the sandstone tower that marks the south side of the entrance to the Chesapeake Bay. The light station, completed in 1792, was deemed unsound 80 years later, due to large cracks on six of the eight walls. A new cast iron tower, built in 1881, stands 350 feet (107 m) from its predecessor. Contrary to the predictions of the inspector and the Lighthouse Board, the sturdy stone edifice did not crumble, nor was it swept into the sea. It stands upright and enduring, and the contrast between the younger and older towers attests to the strength of the past and the innovations of the future.

# SPLIT ROCK

## *Light*

### Minnesota *(1910)*

**⟍ Split Rock Light is actually built** on a 127-foot (39 m) tall cliff known as Stony Point. Split Rock is a river 3 miles (5 km) to the southwest.

**▸▸The light was built after a** storm in 1905 caused the loss of 29 ships and more than 200 deaths.

*A* single blizzard in 1905 damaged 29 of U.S. Steel's carrier fleet. Two vessels wrecked on the rocky north shore of Lake Superior, and not long after the disaster, a delegation headed by the president of the company began lobbying for a lighthouse there. In 1907 Congress responded by appropriating $75,000 for a lighthouse and fog signal. Locally known as Stony Point, the imposing cliff 3 miles (5 km) from the Split Rock River was chosen as the site for the new lighthouse that was completed in 1910. After years of service, the light was placed in the care of the Minnesota Historical Society. The group took over the stewardship of the lighthouse and the 25-acre historic site in 1976.

LOCATION: Minnesota
TOWER HEIGHT: 54 ft. (16 m)
FOCAL PLANE: 168 ft. (51 m)
DAYMARK: Octagonal brick tower with black lantern and gallery
LIGHT CHARACTERISTICS: None
SITE ESTABLISHED: 1910
CURRENT USE: Inactive

LOCATION: North Carolina
TOWER HEIGHT: 100 ft. (30 m)
FOCAL PLANE: 103 ft. (31 m)
DAYMARK: Octagonal white granite tower, black lantern and gallery
LIGHT CHARACTERISTICS: None
SITE ESTABLISHED: 1794
CURRENT USE: Inactive

*Light*

North Carolina *(1817)*

▲ **Built in 1817, Old Baldy is** the oldest lighthouse in North Carolina.

◄◄ **The Bald Head Island Light is 36** feet (11 m) wide and the walls are 5 feet (1.5 m) thick at the base.

*A* haven for rogues, such as Stede Bonnet, the gentleman pirate, and his sometime partner, Blackbeard, the Frying Pan Shoals doomed many ships to a watery grave. Ship captains traveling the waterways called for an official light that could not be hijacked by conniving looters who tried to trap unwary vessels in the waters off Cape Fear. Bald Head Island, named for its smooth south-side dunes that resemble a bare head, was chosen for North Carolina's first lighthouse. The second light constructed at this site still stands and is known as "Old Baldy" to locals. The station has gone in and out of service; the Lighthouse Board tried placing other beacons to better light the treacherous shoals. The mottled tower is maintained by a local nonprofit group and exhibits historical artifacts that illuminate 400 years of the area's maritime history.

▲ **Old Baldy was intermittently** taken out of service as new lighthouses were built on the shores of Bald Head Island. In 1935 it was permanently decommissioned. It was relit in 1985 as an unofficial navigation aid.

▶▶**The light signal of Old Baldy has** changed many times, from a red flash to a Fresnel lens that flashed parallel beams of light to a white fixed light, which was installed in 1903.

# BALD HEAD ISLAND *Light*

▾ **Though Old Baldy is now** checkered with different areas and layers of repair, it was completely white in the 19th century.

▸ **Cape Fear and Bald Head Island** were noted by Europeans like explorer Giovanni da Verrazano, as early as 1524, and, in 1585, the island is mentioned in the logbooks of Sir Walter Raleigh and his colonists.

▸▸ **North Carolina's oldest standing** lighthouse was commissioned by President Thomas Jefferson.

◀ **During World War II, Point** Atkinson was used as a base to help protect Vancouver and its ports.

▶▶**The Point Atkinson Light is at** the end of a 185-acre park of the same name. The park is home to many natural reserves of forests, flowers and animals.

LOCATION: British Columbia
TOWER HEIGHT: 60 ft. (18 m)
FOCAL PLANE: 108 ft. (33 m)
DAYMARK: Octagonal tower with six ribs, lantern and gallery painted white with a red lantern
LIGHT CHARACTERISTICS:
2 white flashes every 5 seconds
SITE ESTABLISHED: 1874
CURRENT USE: Active

# POINT ATKINSON

## *Light*

### British Columbia *(1912)*

*A*lthough other nearby old-growth forests were razed in logging expeditions, navigational necessity preserved the stand of Douglas fir trees behind the lighthouse at Point Atkinson. The dark background of trees contrasted perfectly with the white tower and made it visible to vessels far out at sea. As a result, the picturesque lighthouse is surrounded by ancient sylvan crones, some five centuries old, that stand in awesome monument to times gone by. The current lighthouse was built in 1912, but a light has shone at the point since 1874.

# POINT ATKINSON *Light*

**The Canadian Coast Guard** used the Point Atkinson Light to test different automated lighthouse systems in the 1980s.

**Point Atkinson Light** has been featured in three Hollywood horror movies.

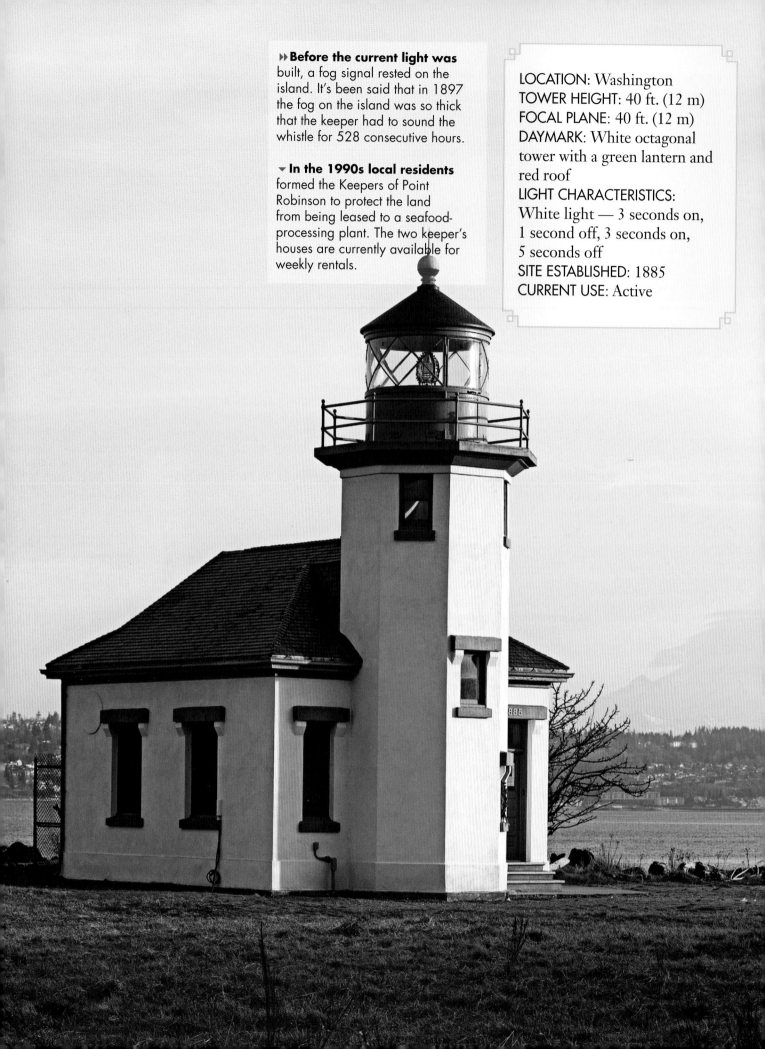

**▸▸Before the current light was** built, a fog signal rested on the island. It's been said that in 1897 the fog on the island was so thick that the keeper had to sound the whistle for 528 consecutive hours.

**▾In the 1990s local residents** formed the Keepers of Point Robinson to protect the land from being leased to a seafood-processing plant. The two keeper's houses are currently available for weekly rentals.

LOCATION: Washington
TOWER HEIGHT: 40 ft. (12 m)
FOCAL PLANE: 40 ft. (12 m)
DAYMARK: White octagonal tower with a green lantern and red roof
LIGHT CHARACTERISTICS: White light — 3 seconds on, 1 second off, 3 seconds on, 5 seconds off
SITE ESTABLISHED: 1885
CURRENT USE: Active

# POINT ROBINSON

*Light*

**Washington** *(1915)*

$\mathcal{B}$uilt in 1915, the Point Robinson Light sits on the halfway mark between Seattle and Tacoma on Maury Island. The light was fitted with a fifth-order Fresnel lens, which still resides in the lantern room today. The fog signal building, erected in 1885, is still there, too, but the signal has since been deactivated. The keeper's houses on the island were built prior to the light, the first in 1885, when the island acted as a fog station, and the second in 1907. With a 38-foot (12 m) tower, the light can be seen 12 miles (19 km) out at sea.

▴ **Although a road has been built to connect** Maury Island with nearby Vashon Island, access to the lighthouse is still only by ferry or private boat.

▸ **The Point Robinson Light was featured in** "The Red Ranger Came Calling," a holiday story written by Berkeley Breathed.

# HARBOUR TOWN

## Light

### South Carolina (1970)

*A* privately financed tourist attraction, Harbour Town Lighthouse is the brainchild of Charles Fraser, who developed Hilton Head Island as a resort community. The lighthouse, built in 1970, is the backdrop to Harbour Town Golf Links and has become the symbol of the exclusive Sea Pines development, as well as the entire Hilton Head area. When visitors climb to the top of the 90-foot (27 m) tower they are afforded a breathtaking view of the harbor, as well as access to the Top of the Lighthouse, a shop that sells souvenirs, jewelry and Hilton Head collectibles.

▴ **Each of the nine landings of the lighthouse have displays** on the history of Hilton Head Island, including topics from colonial history, the Civil War, places to visit, and the resort itself.

▸▸**Though built to attract shoppers to the budding town, rather** than to protect sailors from hazardous seas, the light is listed on navigation maps and shows a white flash every 2.5 seconds.

LOCATION: South Carolina
TOWER HEIGHT: 90 ft. (27 m)
FOCAL PLANE: 90 ft. (27 m)
DAYMARK: Octagonal tower
with horizontal red and white
stripes, red gallery and green
lantern roof
LIGHT CHARACTERISTICS:
White flash every 2.5 seconds
SITE ESTABLISHED: 1970
CURRENT USE: Active

◄◄ **It takes 110 stairs to reach the top of the Harbour** Town Light, where one can see the marina, the Calibogue Sound and even Daufuskie Island.

▼ **In the 1970s many naysayers believed the** lighthouse would be ineffective and nicknamed the tower "Fraser's Folly." Within a decade, however, the light had become the island's trademark.

# BLOCK ISLAND SOUTHEAST

## *Light*

### Rhode Island *(1875)*

*S*aid to be haunted by the disgruntled wife of one of the light's keepers, Block Island Southeast was built in 1875. It housed a first-order Fresnel lens. The light characteristic was changed in 1929 to a flashing green light every 5 seconds. The Block Island Southeast light survived a hurricane in 1938, and the following year a ship was grounded on the shores in front of the light. In 1990 the light was deactivated, but 4 years later, after several renovations and being relocated 300 feet (91 m) inland, it was relit and remains an active aid to navigation.

▲ **The lighthouse can claim a ghostly inhabitant, "Mad Maggie."** Mad Maggie, murdered by her husband, is said to hold a grudge against all men. There have been reports that she has locked male visitors in closets and lifted up their beds to shake them. In one extreme case, she is said to have locked the keeper out of the lighthouse.

▶▶ **Uncommon for lighthouses of its day, the Block Island** Southeast Light's lantern room has 16 sides.

LOCATION: Rhode Island
TOWER HEIGHT: 52 ft. (16 m)
FOCAL PLANE: 258 ft. (79 m)
DAYMARK: Natural foundation
with a black lantern
LIGHT CHARACTERISTICS:
Green flash every 5 seconds
SITE ESTABLISHED: 1875
CURRENT USE: Active

▲ **The light should have been built approximately** 20 years sooner but the Lighthouse Board used the money appropriated for the construction to rebuild the Block Island North Light.

▸▸ **The brick and granite lighthouse, designed in** a melding of Gothic Revival and Italianate styles, is a showpiece of mid-Victorian architecture.

# MUKILTEO

## Light

### Washington *(1906)*

▸▸**The Mukilteo light actually has two** lights in the lantern room, a fixed fourth-order Fresnel lens and a multi-bull's-eye fourth-order Fresnel lens.

▾**Mukilteo is often used for weddings**, and legend has it that no rain has ever fallen on wedding ceremony held there.

One of the few wooden-frame beacons to reach its 100th birthday, the Mukilteo Light Station was built using the design of C.W. Leick and resembles the lighthouses at Ediz Hook and Cape Arago. Named for a Snohomish Indian word for "good camping place," Mulkiteo was the meeting ground for Governor Isaac Stevens and the heads of 22 Puget Sound tribes who came together to create the Treaty of Point Elliot. The lighthouse took up residence about 11 years later and currently sports a fog signal with a remote sensor and a fixed fourth-order Fresnel lens. The local historical society has taken over the care of the light and makes it available for tours and weddings.

LOCATION: Washington
TOWER HEIGHT: 30 ft. (9 m)
FOCAL PLANE: 33 ft. (10 m)
DAYMARK: Octagonal structure
painted white with red roof
LIGHT CHARACTERISTICS:
White flash every 5 seconds
SITE ESTABLISHED: 1906
CURRENT USE: Active

**▲ Since 1906, 18 official keepers** have kept watch at the Mukilteo Light Station. Until electricity was installed in the station in 1927, keepers and their assistants took turns manning 6-hour shifts to keep the light operational 24 hours a day.

**▲ In 1981 a remote fog sensor** based on light-reflection readings was installed in the Mukilteo Light. Unfortunately, the sensor would go off on foggy and clear days alike. It was discovered that the seawall surrounding the tower reflected sunlight, which set off the sensor. The rocks have since been painted black to avoid the problem.

**▸▸ German architect Carl W. Leick** designed the lighthouse.

# KEEPERS OF THE LIGHT

Many lighthouse keepers lived isolated lives, often suffering deprivation and hardship to keep the flame burning for those out on the water. Lighthouses built in remote areas, some even offshore, offered an existence as spare and spartan as the confines of a prison. Where there was fertile soil or a protected patch of land, many keepers established farms and gardens to support their families. Wily cows and gate-hopping goats figure in the folklore of some lights. Keepers lucky enough to be located closer to populated areas enjoyed the benefits of schools and community as well as easier access to the daily necessities of life.

The keeper's most essential work was to fuel and light the flame at the summit of the lighthouse.

Winding the works, polishing the glass to keep it clear of soot, trimming the wick of the lamp to avoid smoke, keeping the lantern room free of leaks and maintaining a sound and solid structure were the tasks that occupied the nights and days of lighthouse keepers. Strenuous in the best of circumstances, the work required Herculean effort during storms. One famous lighthouse lady, Abbie Burgess, at the age of 17, tended the light and cared for her sick mother and two baby sisters for a month while her father, the keeper at Matinicus Rock (an island lighthouse off the coast of Maine) was trapped on the mainland by a winter storm. Characters such as these abound in stories of lighthouse keepers: hearty souls who braved the fury of the elements for the benefit of others.

HARPER'S WEEKLY.

A JOURNAL OF CIVILIZATION

Vol. XIII.—No. 657.]      NEW YORK, SATURDAY, JULY 31, 1869.      [SINGLE COPIES, TEN CENTS. $4.00 PER YEAR IN ADVANCE.

MISS IDA LEWIS, THE HEROINE OF NEWPORT.—PHOT. BY MANCHESTER BROTHERS, PROVIDENCE, R. I.—[SEE PAGE 484.]

◁ **Sixteen-year-old keeper Ida Lewis of Lime Rock,** Rhode Island made her first rescue single handedly in 1858 when she saved four small boys whose boat had capsized in the frigid New England water. Ten years later, Ida rowed a slew of Fort Adams soldiers to safety for which *Harper's Weekly* ran a feature article. Ida went on to receive a silver medal from the Life Saving Benevolent Association, a visit from President Ulysses S. Grant and became the first female to be granted a gold medal for heroism.

◁◁ **The keeper's kitchen in the Old Point Loma** Lighthouse, San Diego, California. When a new light went up at Point Loma in 1891, lightkeeper Robert Israel moved his family from Old Point Loma to the new station. As part of the Cabrillo National Monument, the old lighthouse was turned over to the National Park Service in 1933. In the early 1980s, the park service meticulously restored the old light, furnishing the living quarters to look as they did when Israel tended the light.

▽ **American lighthouse keeper, Fannie May** Salter manned the lens of Turkey Point Light on the Chesapeake Bay for over 20 years. While performing the duties of keeper, Fannie raised three children, farmed vegetables and tended to sheep and fowl. She is one of four women who throughout history have maintained Turkey Point Light.

Not every lighthouse keeper lived a life of drudgery and solitude. John Paul Rademuller, whose ghost is said to roam the grounds at Gibraltar Point Light, was a great favorite with the folks in Toronto. He brewed and sold his own beer, as well as hosting gatherings in the lighthouse where he treated locals to rounds of homemade ale. Captain Mills O. Burnham was keeper at Cape Canaveral for 33 years and entertained guests at numerous parties at the light. The Burnhams owned one of the few pianos in the vicinity and social events at the beacon, including the lighthouse balls, attracted crowds of visitors from the mainland. These and other gregarious keepers found ways to combine festivity with a demanding and often lonely occupation.

**The number of paranormal occurrences** at some American lighthouses may convince — or at least intrigue — even the most skeptical of visitors. In far-reaching locales, lighthouses seem to be prime territory for the ghosts of forlorn lovers, murder victims, devoted keepers and suicides.

### Heceta Head, Oregon

The apparition at Heceta Head Light is well known. Since the 1950s, every keeper has reported strange occurrences, such as screams in the night and objects changing positions. Since the ghost, called Rue, has been seen looking out the attic window and walking near the lighthouse around the grave of a baby, it is believed that she is the infant's mother. One of the more notable happenings occurred in the 1970s when a worker claimed to have seen Rue in the attic. While working outside, he accidentally broke the attic window and refused to go inside to clean it up for fear of the ghost. A coworker went in to investigate and found the glass swept into a pile.

*"A Ghost — Somebody tried last Thursday night to get up a ghost at the fort, but it was a failure. Lots of people went there about 9 o'clock at night; but the ghost didn't amount to much ... We don't think much of these sham ghosts. If they could get up a real bonifide ghost, such as we read about, there would be some fun in it and everybody would go and see it."*

— *St. Augustine Star*, January 4, 1872

## St. Augustine, Florida

St. Augustine's Light is considered a hotspot of paranormal activity, and one paranormal investigation team had a firsthand experience of hearing a woman's voice call out "Help me"; even better, they got it on tape. People have claimed to hear footsteps running up and down the stairs and the voice of an adolescent girl. A padlocked door mysteriously opens without tripping the alarm, and several visitors report visions of a ghost in the basement. Though these ghost stories may seem too disparate to be taken seriously, historical records of a family that died during the construction of the lighthouse and one hanged keeper may lend some credence to the tales.

## Owl's Head, Maine

The ghosts that haunt Owl's Head Light seem to be relatively friendly, with activity such as doors slamming and a female apparition rattling silverware. Footprints have been found in the snow, and the temperature in the keeper's house always mysteriously fluctuates. Other times, the ghost has been known to polish the brass in the light tower. One story states that a little girl woke up in the middle of the night and explained to her parents that the foghorn needed to be turned on. The girl had been informed of this necessity by a vision who resembled an old sea captain.

## New London Ledge Lighthouse, Connecticut

The sad story of a love gone wrong, the apparition nicknamed "Ernie" found that his wife had run off with a ferry captain while he was out getting supplies for the lighthouse. When Ernie returned and found his wife gone, he threw himself off the gallery of the tower. Keepers and visitors to the lighthouse have noticed doors open and close, covers pulling themselves off beds, knocks on bedroom doors in the middle of the night and strange noises and whispers at all times of the day. One fisherman supposedly found his boat untied after claiming he thought the ghost was a hoax. Keepers and their families have reportedly seen Ernie in various rooms of the house.

*"Died on the evening of the 2nd of January, J.P. Radan Muller, keeper of the lighthouse on Gibraltar Point. From circumstances there is moral proof of his having been murdered. If the horrid crime admits of aggravation when the inoffensive and benevolent character of the unfortunate sufferer are considered, his murder will be pronounced most barbarous and inhuman. The parties lost with him are the proposed perpetrators and are in prison."*

— *York Gazette*, January 14, 1815

## Peggy's Cove, Nova Scotia

Peggy's Cove in Nova Scotia has several accounts of a "lady in blue" seen walking along the edge of a cliff looking ready to jump. Some people claim to even have heard her speak, but Canada's real paranormal gem is Gibraltar Point.

## Gibraltar Point, Ontario

Legend has it that the first light keeper of Gibraltar Point, one of Toronto's oldest buildings, was murdered in 1815 by three soldiers to whom he refused to serve beer. The keeper, John Rademuller, was supposedly a bootlegger who smuggled beer in from the United States. According to folklore, the soldiers threw him off the lighthouse and then cut his body into pieces, which they buried separately around the island. In 1893 a light keeper dug up a coffin and found a human jawbone. Visitors and keepers alike have been known to see an apparition of a man wandering the grounds; it's believed Rademuller is out looking for his scattered body parts. There are also accounts of strange noises, sounding like something being dragged, and footsteps on the stairs.

# *Skeletal*
## CONSTRUCTION

### BUILDERS OF MODERN LIGHT
towers most often choose the skeletal form. Towers consist of a central cylinder surrounded by four to eight slanting columns. Lighthouses of this style are prefabricated and assembled on site. Many skeletal towers serve as range lighthouses, a pair of light towers that align to guide ships on a proper course through tricky waterways. At 191 feet (58 m), Cape Charles Lighthouse (built in 1895) ranks as the tallest skeletal lighthouse in the United States. The oldest, Whitefish Point Light — built in 1861 as an experiment — still stands. These types of towers were highly favored by Congress around the turn of the 20th century, as their construction costs were about half those of a traditional stone tower. Early construction materials of wood and then cast iron were soon supplanted by steel for later towers. Other notable examples of lights with skeletal construction include Marblehead in Massachusetts, Coney Island Light in New York and Sanibel Island Light in Florida.

◀ **American Shoal Lighthouse**
on Sugarloaf Key, Florida

# WHITEFISH POINT

## *Light*

### Michigan *(1861)*

The oldest active light on Lake Superior, Whitefish Point Light has a steel framework that battles the strong winds of the area with a streamlined grace. The tower, although utilitarian and modern in appearance, was actually built in 1861. The marker at the site states that "the point marks the course change for ore boats and other ships navigating this treacherous coastline to and from St. Mary's Canal." The current structure at Whitefish Point was preceded by a 65-foot (20 m) stone tower completed in 1849. This light was quickly replaced in response to the boom in maritime traffic caused by the new lock at Sault Ste. Marie.

▲ **In 1975, the light at Whitefish Point went out for an** unknown reason and one ship, the *Edmund Fitzgerald,* met its demise. Every year on the anniversary of the wreck, a memorial service at the light station honors the crew of the ship and all mariners who were lost on the Great Lakes.

▶▶ **A fog signal was added to the Whitefish Point Light in** 1875 to help ships navigate the fierce fog off Lake Superior.

LOCATION: Michigan
TOWER HEIGHT: 76 ft. (23 m)
FOCAL PLANE: 80 ft. (24 m)
DAYMARK: Pyramidal white skeletal tower with center cylinder, double gallery and red lantern roof
LIGHT CHARACTERISTICS: 2 white flashes 5 seconds apart, every 20 seconds
SITE ESTABLISHED: 1848
CURRENT USE: Active

◀◀ **The Coast Guard automated the** Whitefish Point Light in 1971. Its light signs two white flashes, 5 seconds apart, every 20 seconds.

▼ **Across from the Light Station sits** the Whitefish Point Bird Observatory, and most of the park serves as a state-sanctioned wildlife sanctuary.

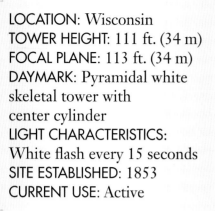

LOCATION: Wisconsin
TOWER HEIGHT: 111 ft. (34 m)
FOCAL PLANE: 113 ft. (34 m)
DAYMARK: Pyramidal white
skeletal tower with
center cylinder
LIGHT CHARACTERISTICS:
White flash every 15 seconds
SITE ESTABLISHED: 1853
CURRENT USE: Active

**▾ The tower was relocated to** Twin Rivers Point in 1894 after being exhibited at the World's Fair in Chicago the previous year. The base of the previous tower was left and built into the keeper's house.

**▸▸ Electricity was installed in 1920** with a third-order Fresnel lens. The lens remained in action in the tower until 1952, when it broke. A modern optic has since taken its place.

# RAWLEY POINT

*Light*

Wisconsin *(1853)*

$\mathscr{B}$efore a brick tower was erected on Rawley Point, 26 ships met sorry fates on its rocks. The worst tragedy occurred in 1887, when the steamship *Vernon* sank, taking 36 crew members and passengers with her. The light tower, along with an accompanying keeper's house, served mariners until 1894, when a steel tower was built to replace the old brick one. The new tower, which hails from the Chicago World's Fair of 1893, still stands. Its skeletal structure resists the high winds that whip the coast of Lake Michigan. Rawley Point Light is the second tallest in Wisconsin and one of the brightest; its beams are visible as far as 19 miles (31 km) away.

# MARBLEHEAD

## *Light*

### Massachusetts *(1835)*

*O*n a yachting resort town populated by Victorian villas, a cast iron lighthouse is something of an oddity. The only lighthouse of this style in New England, the skeletal-frame beacon at Marblehead replaced a small tower with a beam that became obstructed when summer cottages proliferated in the area in the 1870s. Jane C. Martin, the second keeper at Marblehead, was one of the rare women to hold this position during the early 19th century. Today Marblehead is still bustling with sailing vessels that mark their course by the light of the faithful sentinel at the head of the harbor.

▲ **Though the Marblehead Light has had a green fixed** light since 1938, it was originally a fixed red light.

▸▸**During World War II, the U.S. Army used the light as a** station, and it was off-limits to the public from 1941 to 1946.

LOCATION: Massachusetts
TOWER HEIGHT: 105 ft. (32 m)
FOCAL PLANE: 130 ft. (40 m)
DAYMARK: Pyramidal brown
skeletal tower, black lantern
and black double gallery
LIGHT CHARACTERISTICS:
Fixed green light
SITE ESTABLISHED: 1835
CURRENT USE: Active

LOCATION: South Carolina
TOWER HEIGHT: 94 ft. (29 m)
FOCAL PLANE: 136 ft. (41 m)
DAYMARK: White skeletal cast
iron tower with center cylinder
LIGHT CHARACTERISTICS:
Fixed sodium vapor light
(decorative)
SITE ESTABLISHED: 1877
CURRENT USE: Inactive

**▲ Union soldiers built the first light on Hilton Head** during the Civil War. When it was destroyed in 1869, Congress authorized the building of the Hilton Head Range lights, though they were not completed until 1881.

**◀◀ Legend has it that the ghost of one of the keeper's** daughters, Caroline, haunts the lighthouse on rainy nights, wearing a blue dress. In 1898 during a fierce storm, Caroline found her father dying from a heart attack in the lantern room; though she couldn't save him, she kept the light going.

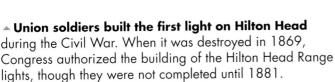

$\mathscr{A}$ hexagonal, pyramidal tower, the Hilton Head is a range rear light. Ranges are lights that work together to assist in navigation. They are positioned so that when a vessel is sailing the correct course through a dangerous waterway the range rear light appears to be directly over the range front light. In the case of Hilton Head, the range front light was torn down, and only its larger partner still stands. The light has been decommissioned and is now privately owned but still open to visitors by appointment.

# HILTON HEAD RANGE REAR

## *Light*

**South Carolina** *(1881)*

# SANIBEL ISLAND

## *Light*

### Florida *(1884)*

$\mathcal{T}$he citizens of the first settlement on Sanibel Island recognized the need for a light on their seashell-littered shores in the 1830s. Repeated requests from locals and numerous recommendations from the Lighthouse Board prodded Congress to eventually appropriate funding, and the tower was finally lit in 1884. The construction was not without difficulty, though. Most of the iron segments of the current tower had to be fished from the bottom of the sea after the ship carrying building materials for the beacon sank off the very coast it was meant to protect. The light was automated in 1949, and city employees currently maintain and supervise the grounds.

▲ **The central column of the Sanibel Island Light is 10 feet** (3 m) off the ground and is accessible by an external staircase.

▶▶ **Henry Shanahan and his children were keepers of the** Sanibel Island Light on and off from 1892 to 1941. At one point as many as 13 children in the extended family helped to run the lighthouse.

LOCATION: Florida
TOWER HEIGHT: 102 ft. (31 m)
FOCAL PLANE: 98 ft. (30 m)
DAYMARK: Pyramidal brown
skeletal tower with center
cylinder
LIGHT CHARACTERISTICS:
2 white flashes every 6 seconds
SITE ESTABLISHED: 1884
CURRENT USE: Active

▲ **The light received indoor** plumbing in 1923, the same year it began using acetylene gas.

▸ **The Sanibel Island Light had** a third-order Fresnel lens installed when it was first erected in 1884.

▸▸ **The open skeletal design** of the Sanibel Island Light was used because it was believed that it would allow high winds and storms to pass through without damage.

▲ **It was possible to watch NASA** launches on Cape Canaveral in the 1960s and 1970s from the spiral staircase in the lighthouse.

◀ **Sanibel Island had a persistent** mosquito problem, making for barely tolerable conditions. The keepers and their families went out in bee nets and gloves, houses had screened porches and insect repellent was generously employed.

◀◀ **Before the roadway to the** island was completed in 1963 the only way on and off the island was a 3-mile (5 km) ferry ride.

# THE FUTURE OF LIGHTHOUSES

**Lighthouses suffered in the advent of automation.**
Without the staffing of a keeper many were abandoned
to slow deterioration. Radar and radio towers, and the
Global Positioning System (GPS) further relegated
beacons to obsolescence, and vandalism and neglect
plagued lights that were decommissioned. The Coast
Guard, better served by lights carried on large buoys and
steel towers, soon began demolishing the buildings that
had fallen into disrepair.

An outcry arose from many local citizens when their
region's beacon was threatened with destruction. Groups
like Save the Light, a grassroots nonprofit in South
Carolina, organized to protect and preserve the sentinels
that had guarded the coasts so steadfastly. All across

◄ **The Lighthouse Automation and**
Modernization Program (LAMP) was founded
in the 1960s. Automation eliminated the need
for lighthouse keepers and by 1990 all U.S.
lighthouses were automated with the exception of
the Boston Harbor Island Light in Massachusetts.
The Pemaquid Point Light (shown to the left) was
automated as early as 1934.

North America hundreds of initiatives raised millions of dollars to restore and maintain these important links to the past.

The transfer of lighthouses to local preservation societies has been aided by the National Historic Lighthouse Preservation Act of 2000. This act provides a mechanism for the federal government to release the care and ownership of lighthouses to state and local governments, nonprofit corporations, educational agencies and community development organizations. Under the act such organizations must be financially capable of maintaining the light station and must make it available to the general public for purposes of education or recreation.

As the understanding of the cultural importance of lighthouses becomes more widespread, and many lights are preserved and protected, people have greater access to the historic stations that may have guided the vessels of their forefathers. In some cases the preservation groups that maintain lighthouses have established museums on the grounds. Exhibits document important innovations and historical developments. In lighthouses like the Pemaquid Point Light in Maine and the St. Simons Island Light in Georgia, Fresnel lenses still focus the lamp's beams. Now solar panels provide a sustainable and environmentally friendly power source for many beacons. Championed by grassroots support, and serving the community through education, many lights may enjoy a future as bright as their past.

▲ **Global Positioning System (GPS) is a satellite-** based navigation system. It uses 24 satellites put into orbit by the U.S. Department of Defense. Originally intended for military use only, GPS was made available to civilians in 1983.

▶ **After most of the U.S. lighthouses were** automated in the 1960s, navigational buoys began replacing lightships in the 1970s.

▲ **Many active lighthouses today are powered by solar** energy. This cost-effective, energy-efficient source of energy keeps maintaining the lighthouses simple and easy.

▸ **Starting in the 1980s, the U.S. Coast Guard began** replacing classical Fresnel lenses with aerobeacons or acrylic lenses though many lighthouses still house their original lenses. The St. Simon Lighthouse (pictured right) still operates with its original third-order Fresnel lens.

# THE STATUE OF LIBERTY

*"We will not forget that liberty here made her home; nor shall her chosen altar be neglected."*

— President Grover Cleveland on accepting the Statue of Liberty

**The Statue of Liberty** has welcomed millions of immigrants to the United States since 1886. The towering copper-sheathed structure, recognized as a symbol of hope and opportunity, was intended as a navigational aid for New York Harbor. After working the kinks out of the electrical system, engineers were able to illuminate Lady Liberty's torch, and her light could be seen 24 miles (39 km) out to sea.

The practical application of electricity was still a novelty in the late 19th century, and the Statue of Liberty was the first lighthouse to use this new source of power. Ongoing funds to keep the lamp going were not approved initially, and the torch went dark for 2 weeks after the unveiling of the statue. President Grover Cleveland secured monies through an executive order, and Lady Liberty was placed under the care of the Lighthouse Board.

The light, never considered a highly effective aid to navigation, was decommissioned in 1902. At this point the U.S. War Department assumed responsibility for the maintenance of the statue. Finally, in 1933, the National Park Service took up the care of this historic landmark and opened it to the public. Major renovations to the structure in the mid-1980s strengthened the internal architecture and patched holes in the copper skin. Although visitors can no longer climb to the top of Lady Liberty, her pedestal houses a museum that details the history and construction of the monument, as well as exhibiting the original torch.

▼ **The Statue of Liberty was** a gift of friendship from France to the United States in honor of the centennial anniversary of independence. Frédéric Auguste Bartholdi and Gustave Eiffel, who would later build the Eiffel Tower, designed the statue. Almost 10 years after July 4, 1876, Lady Liberty was dedicated on October 28, 1886.

# LIBERTY'S BURNING *Torch*

◄ **After several failed attempts at** lighting Lady Liberty, the torch was equipped with nine electric arc lamps while five lamps were installed on the ground. The torch lights could be seen 24 miles (39 km) out at sea. In November 1886, the Statue of Liberty became an operational lighthouse. Despite its difficulty in lighting the New York Harbor, the Statue of Liberty remained an aid to navigation until 1902 when it was deactivated.

▼ **Lady Liberty's torch and the arm** that holds it arrived in New York in 1885, 9 years after Frédéric Bartholdi completed it. The torch was changed several times during the statue's days as a lighthouse, but a team from the National Park Service restored it to its original glory in 1984. The new torch was made of copper with a gold-leaf coating. The original torch can be viewed in the lobby of the monument.

▲ **The Statue of Liberty wasn't** always green. It is made of copper, but oxidation, a chemical reaction between copper and air, turned the statue its pale green over time.

◄ **The Statue of Liberty arrived in** New York as 350 pieces packed in 214 crates and was constructed onsite.

◀ **The Statue of Liberty was** originally intended to arrive in the United States in 1876 for the official centennial, but fundraising problems in both France and the United States caused almost 10 years of delays. In France, they held a lottery and sold signed clay models of the statue. The United States had agreed to build Lady Liberty's pedestal; however, funds were low. Joseph Pulitzer through his newspaper, the *New York World*, stepped in and asked the *World*'s readership to donate to the cause, promising to publish the name of all the contributors in the newspaper.

*"Give me your tired, your poor,*
*Your huddled masses yearning to breathe free,*
*The wretched refuse of your teeming shore.*
*Send these, the homeless, tempest-tost to me,*
*I lift my lamp beside the golden door!"*

*— From "New Colossus," the sonnet by Emma Lazarus*
*engraved on the pedestal of the Statue of Liberty*

▶ **In 1924 President Calvin Coolidge declared the Statue** of Liberty a national monument. It was administered by the War Department until 1933 when the Department of the Interior took over the area surrounding the monument while the army maintained the island. In 1937 the statue was officially handed over to the National Park Service, a division of the Department of the Interior.

# LIST OF NORTH AMERICAN LIGHTS

## UNITED STATES

### ALABAMA

Mobile Middle Bay
Mobile Point Range Rear Light
Sand Island

### ALASKA

Cape Decision
Cape Hinchinbrook
Cape Sarichef
Eldred Rock
Five Finger Islands
Guard Islands
Mary Island
Odiak Pharos
Point Retreat
Sentinel Island
Tree Point

### CALIFORNIA

Alcatraz Island
Anacapa Island
Battery Point (Crescent City)
Cape Mendocino (old)
Carquinez Strait
East Brother Island
Farallon Island
Fort Point
Lime Point
Los Angeles Harbor
Mile Rocks
Oakland Harbor
Piedras Blancas
Pigeon Point
Point Arena
Point Loma (new)
Point Loma (old)
Point Montara
Point Piños
Point Reyes
Point Sur

▸ **Point Montara,** California

Point Vicente
Punta Gorda
San Luis Obispo
Santa Barbara
Santa Cruz Memorial
Santa Cruz (Walton Breakwater)
Southampton Shoals
St. George Reef
Table Bluff
Trinidad Memorial (replica)
Trinidad Head
Yerba Buena Island

## CONNECTICUT

Avery Point
Faulkners Island
Great Captain Island
Lynde Point
Morgan Point
Mystic Seaport
New London Harbor
New London Ledge
Peck Ledge
Penfield Reef
Saybrook Breakwater
Sheffield Island
Southwest Ledge (New Haven Breakwater)
Stamford Harbor (Chatham Rocks)
Stonington Harbor
Stratford Point
Stratford Shoal
Tongue Point

## DELAWARE

Bellevue Range Rear Light (old)
Bellevue Range Rear Light (new)
Brandywine Shoal
Delaware Breakwater
Fenwick Island
Fourteen Foot Bank
Harbor of Refuge (South) Breakwater
Liston Range Rear Light
Liston Front Range Light

◀ **Old Point Loma,** California

▲ **Boca Chita,** Florida

Marcus Hook Range Rear Light
Mispillion (old)
Reedy Island Range Rear Light

FLORIDA

Alligator Reef
Amelia Island
American Shoal
Anclote Key
Boca Chita
Boca Grande Rear Range Light
Cape Canaveral
Cape Florida (Cape Braggs)

Cape San Blas
Cape St. George
Carysfort Reef
Crooked River (Carrabelle)
Dry Tortugas
Egmont Key
Fort Jefferson
Fowey Rocks
Gasparilla Island (Boca Grande)
Hillsboro Inlet
Jupiter Inlet
Key West
Mayport
Northwest Passage (ruins)

Pensacola
Ponce de Leon Inlet
Sand Key
Sanibel Island
Seahorse Key (Cedar Keys)
Sombrero Key
St. Augustine
St. Johns River
St. Joseph Point
St. Marks Range Rear

## GEORGIA

Cockspur Island
Little Cumberland Island
Sapelo Island
Sapelo Island Front Range Light
St. Simons Island
Tybee Island

## HAWAII

Cape Kumukahi
Diamond Head
Hiiumaa House
Kauhola Point
Kilauea Point
Lahaina
Makapuu Point
McGregor Point
Molokai-Kalaupapa
Nawiliwili Harbor

## ILLINOIS

Chicago Harbor
Chicago Harbor Southeast Guidewall
Grosse Point
Waukegan Harbor

## INDIANA

Buffington Breakwater
Calumet Harbor
Gary Breakwater

▲ **Grosse Point**, Illinois

◀◀ **St. Marks**, Florida

Indiana Harbor East Breakwater
Michigan City (old)
Michigan City Pierhead
Michigan City Breakwater

## LOUISIANA

Chandeleur Island
Frank's Island
Madisonville Lighthouse
New Canal
Pass a l'outre
Pass Manchac

Point au Fer Reef
Port Pontchartrain
Sabine Pass
South Pass Range Lights
Southwest Pass Entrance
Southwest Reef
Tchefuncte River Range Rear Light

## MAINE

Bass Harbor Head
Bear Island
Blue Hill Bay

▲ **Chatham,** Massachusetts

◀ **Cape Elizabeth Light East,** Maine

Ram Island Ledge
Ram Island
Rockland Harbor Breakwater
Rockland Harbor Southwest
Saddleback Ledge
Seguin Island
Spring Point Ledge
Squirrel Point
Tenants Harbor
Two Bush Island
West Quoddy Head
Whaleback Ledge

Whitehead Island
Whitlock's Mill
Winter Harbor
Wood Island

## MARYLAND

Bloody Point Bar
Cedar Point
Concord Point (Havre de Grace)
Cove Point
Craighill Channel Lower Range Lights
Cutoff Channel Upper Range

Cutoff Channel Lower Range
Drum Point
Fishing Battery
Fort Carroll
Fort Washington
Hooper Island
Hooper Strait
Lazaretto Point
Piney Point
Point Lookout (old)
Point No Point
Pooles Island
Sandy Point Shoal
Seven Foot Knoll
Sharps Island
Solomons Lump
Thomas Point Shoal
Turkey Point

## MASSACHUSETTS

Annisquam Harbor
Bass River
Bird Island
Borden Flats
Boston Harbor
Brant Point
Brant Point (old)
Butler Flats
Buzzards Bay Entrance
Cape Ann (Thatcher Island)
Cape Cod (Highland)
Cape Poge (Pogue)
Chatham
Clarks Point
Cleveland East Ledge
Deer Island
Derby Whar
Dog Bar Breakwater
Duxbury Pier ("Bug")
East Chop (Telegraph Hill)
Eastern Point
Edgartown Harbor
Fort Pickering (Winter Island)
Gay Head
The Graves
Hospital Point (Range Front)
Hyannis (Range Rear)

Long Island Head
Long Point
Marblehead
Minots Ledge
Monomoy Point
Nauset Beach
Ned's Point
Newburyport Harbor (Plum Island)
Newburyport Harbor Range Light
Nobska Point
Palmer Island
Plymouth (Gurnet)
Point Gammon
Race Point
Sandy Neck
Sankaty Head
Scituate
Stage Harbor
Straitsmouth Island
Tarpaulin Cove
Ten Pound Island
Three Sisters
West Chop
Wings Neck
Wood End

## MICHIGAN

Alpena
Au Sable Point
Beaver Island
Beaver Head
Big Bay Point
Big Sable Point (Grand Point au Sable)
Bois Blanc Island (old)
Cedar River Rear Range Light
Charity Island
Charlevoix South Pier
Cheboygan Crib
Cheboygan River Range Front Light
Copper Harbor
Copper Harbor Rear Range Light
Crisp Point
Detour Reef
Detroit River (Bar Point Shoal)
Eagle Harbor

▶▶ **Ludington,** Michigan

▼ **Point Betsie,** Michigan

▲ **South Haven,** Michigan

McGulpin's Point
Mendota (Bete Grise)
Menominee (North Pier)
Middle Island
Minneapolis Shoal
Mission Point (old)
Munising Front Range Light
Munising Rear Range Light
Muskegon South Breakwater
Muskegon South Pierhead
North Manitou Shoal
Ontonagon
Ontonagon West Pierhead
Passage Island
Peche Island Rear Range
Peninsula Point
Pentwater North Breakwater
Pentwater South Breakwater
Petoskey Pierhead
Pipe Island
Poe Reef
Point Betsie
Point Iroquois

Pointe aux Barques
Port Austin Reef
Port Sanilac
Portage River (Jacobsville)
Poverty Island
Presque Isle (new)
Presque Isle (old)
Presque Isle Harbor Breakwater
Presque Isle Front Range
Presque Isle Rear Range
Robert Manning Memorial
Rock Harbor
Rock of Ages
Round Island
Round Island (St. Mary's River)
Round Island Passage
Saginaw River (Range Rear)
Sand Hills
Sand Point (Baraga)
Sand Point (Escanaba)
Seul Choix Pointe
Skillagalee (Ile aux Galets)
South Fox Island

Old Field Point, New York

Fort Niagara, New York

South Haven South Pierhead
South Manitou Island
Spectacle Reef
Squaw Island
St. Clair Flats South Channel Range Light
St. Helena Island
St. Joseph North Pier
St. Martin Island
St. Mary River Upper Range Rear Light
Stannard Rock
Stoneport

Sturgeon Point
Tawas Point (Ottawa Point)
Thunder Bay Island
Waugoshance
White River
White Shoal
Whitefish Point
Windmill Point

▲ **Warrior Rock,** Oregon

◄◄ **Umpqua River,** Oregon

## MINNESOTA

Duluth Harbor North Breakwater
Duluth South Breakwater
Grand Marais
Minneapolis Point
Split Rock

Two Harbors
Two Harbors East Breakwater

## MISSISSIPPI

Biloxi
Round Island
Ship Island

## MISSOURI

Mark Twain Memorial (replica)

## NEW HAMPSHIRE

Burkehaven
Herrick Cove
Isle of Shoals (White Island)
Loon Island
Portsmouth Harbor (Newcastle)

## NEW JERSEY

Absecon
Barnegat
Cape May Point
Chapel Hill Range Rear
Conover Beacon
East Point (Maurice River)
Elbow of Cross Ledge

Finns Point Range Rear Light
Hereford Inlet (Old)
Miah Maull Shoal
Navesink Twin
Sandy Hook
Sea Girt
Ship John Shoal
Tinicum Island Range Rear Light
Tuckers Island (replica)

## NEW YORK

Bluff Point
Braddock Point
Brewerton Rear Range Light
Buffalo (Main)
Buffalo Crib

▾ **Watch Hill,** Rhode Island

New Dorp (Swash Channel Range Rear Light)
North Dumpling
North Brother Island
Ogdensburg Harbor
Old Field Point
Old Orchard Shoal
Orient Point
Oswego Harbor West Pierhead
Plum Island (Plum Gut)
Point aux Roches
Princes Bay (old)
Race Rock
Robbins Reef
Rochester Harbor
Rock Island
Romer Shoal
Rondout Creek (Kingston)
Roosevelt Island
Sacketts Harbor (Horse Island)
Sands Point (old)
Saugerties
Selkirk (Salmon River)
Sodus
Sodus Point
South Buffalo North Side
South Buffalo South Side
Split Rock Point (old)
Staten Island (Range Rear Light)
Statue of Liberty
Stepping Stones
Stony Point (Henderson)
Stony Point
Sunken Rock
Sylvan Beach
Tarrytown (Kingsland Point)
Thirty Mile Point (old)
Three Sisters Island
Tibbets Point
Titanic Memorial
West Bank (Range Front)

◂◂ **Yaquina Bay,** Oregon

▸ **Vermilion,** Ohio

## NORTH CAROLINA

Bodie Island
Cape Hatteras
Cape Lookout
Currituck Beach
Oak Island
Ocracoke Island
Price's Creek (Ruin)
Roanoke River

## OHIO

Ashtabula Harbor
Cedar Point
Celina (See Rotary)
Cleveland Harbor Pierhead East
Cleveland Harbor Pierhead West
Cleveland Harbor East Entrance
Conneaut West Breakwater
Fairport West Breakwater
Fairport Harbor
Grand Lake St. Mary's
Huron Harbor
Lorain
Lorain East Breakwater
Manhattan Front Range Light
Manhattan Rear Range Light
Marblehead (Sandusky)
Perry Memorial
Port Clinton
Rotary
South Bass Island
Toledo Harbor
Turtle Island
Vermilion (replica)
West Sister Island

## OREGON

Cape Arago (Cape Gregory)
Cape Blanco
Cape Meares
Cleft of the Rock
Coquille River (Bandon)
Heceta Head
Pelican Bay
Tillamook Rock

Umpqua River
Warrior Rock
Yaquina Bay (old)
Yaquina Head

## PENNSYLVANIA

Erie Harbor North Pierhead
Erie Land (Old Presque Isle)
Presque Isle
Turtle Rock

## RHODE ISLAND

Beavertail
Block Island (North)
Block Island (Southeast)
Bristol Ferry
Castle Hill
Conanicut Island (old)
Conimicut Shoal
Dutch Island
Fuller Rock (ruins)
Hog Island Shoal
Ida Lewis Rock (Lime Rock)
Nayatt Point
Newport Harbor (Goat Island)
Plum Beach
Point Judith
Pomham Rocks (old)
Poplar Point (Wickford Harbor)
Prudence Island (Sandy Point)
Rose Island
Sakonnet
Warwick
Watch Hill

## SOUTH CAROLINA

Bloody Point Range Lights
Cape Romain
Georgetown
Haig Point (Range Rear)
Harbour Town (Hilton Head / Sea Pines)
Hilton Head Range Rear (Leamington)
Hunting Island

▸▸ **Point Wilson,** Washington

Morris Island (Charleston)
Sullivan's Island

## TEXAS

Aransas Pass
Galveston Jetty
Half Moon Reef
Lydia Ann (Aransas Pass)
Matagorda Island
Point Bolivar
Port Isabel (Point Isabel)
Sabine Bank

## VERMONT

Burlington Harbor Breakwater
Colchester Reef
Isle la Motte (old)
Windmill Point (old)

## VIRGINIA

Assateague
Cape Charles
Cape Henry (old)
Cape Henry (new)
Chesapeake (Texas Tower)
Jones Point
New Point Comfort
Newport News Middle Ground
Old Point Comfort
Smith Point
Thimble Shoal
Wolf Trap

## WASHINGTON

Admiralty Head
Alki Point
Brown's Point
Burrows Island
Cape Disappointment
Cape Flattery
Cattle Point (Friday Harbor)
Destruction Island

◄ **Alki Point,** Washington

Dofflemeyer Point
Ediz Harbor
Gig Harbor
Grays Harbor (Westport)
Lime Kiln
Marrowstone Point
Mukilteo
New Dungeness
North Head
Point No Point
Point Robinson
Point Wilson
Skunk Bay
Slip Point
Turn Point
Waadah Island
West Point

## WISCONSIN

Algoma Pierhead
Ashland Harbor Breakwater
Asylum Bay
Calumet Harbor
Cana Island
Chambers Island
Chequamegon Point
Columbia Park
Devils Island
Eagle Bluff
Fond du Lac
Grassy Island Range
Green Bay Harbor Entrance
Kenosha (Southport)
Kenosha Pierhead
Kevich
Kewaunee Pierhead
La Pointe (Long Island)
Longtail Point
Manitowoc Breakwater
Michigan Island (first)
Michigan Island (second)
Milwaukee Breakwater
Milwaukee Pierhead
Neenah
North Point (Milwaukee)
Outer Island
Peshtigo Reef

Pilot Island
Plum Island Range Lights
Port Washington Breakwater
Port Washington (old)
Pottawatomie (Rock Island)
Racine Harbor
Raspberry Island
Sheboygan Breakwater
Sherwood Point
Sturgeon Bay Canal
Sturgeon Bay Ship Canal North Pierhead
Superior Harbor Entry South Breakwater
Two Rivers
Wind Point
Wisconsin Point

▸▸ **Wind Point,** Wisconsin

# CANADA

## ALBERTA

Sylvan Lake

## BRITISH COLUMBIA

Active Pass
Addenbroke Island
Albert Head
Amphitrite Point
Ballenas Island
Bare Point
Barrett Rock
Berens Island
Boat Bluff
Bonilla Island
Brockton Point
Cape Mudge
Cape Beale
Cape Scott
Cape St. James
Capilano
Carmanah Point
Chatham Point
Chrome Island
Discovery Island
Dryad Point
East Point
Egg Island
Entrance Island
Estevan Point
Fiddle Reef
Fisgard
Gallows Point
Green Island
Holland Rock
Ivory Island
Langara Point
Lawyer Island
Lennard Island
Lucy Island

◀ **Sylvan Lake,** Alberta

▶▶ **Cape Mudge,** British Columbia

▲ **Race Rocks,** British Columbia

◄◄ **Big Shippagan,** Nova Scotia

McInnes Island
Merry Island
Nootka
North Sand Heads
Pachena Point
Pine Island
Point Atkinson
Pointer Island
Porlier Pass
Portlock Point
Prospect Point
Pulteney Point
Quatsino, Kains Island
Race Rocks
Sand Heads
Saturna Island
Scarlett Point
Sheringham
Sisters Rocks/Islet
South Sand Heads
Trial Island

Triangle Island
Triple Island

## MANITOBA

Black Bear Island
George Island
Gimli
Gull Harbour
Red River Range
Warren Landing Lower Range Front
Warren Landing Upper Range Rear

## NEW BRUNSWICK

Bayswater
Belyeas Point
Big Shippagan
Black Point
Bliss Island
Bouctouche Bar

▲ **Long Point,** New Brunswick

Campbellton Wharf Range Back Light
Cap-Des-Caissie Point
Cape Enrage
Cape Spencer
Cape Tourmentine Pier Range Light
Caraquet Range
The Cedars
Chance Harbour
Cherry Islet
Cocagne Range Front  Light
Deer Point
Dixon Point
Drew's Head
Fanjoy's Point
Fort Monckton
Gagetown
Gannet Rock
Great Duck Island
Hampstead
Head Harbour
Huestis Island (Lower Jemseg)
Inch Arron Point Range Front
Indian Point Front Range Light

Indian Point Range Light (Tourmentine)
Jouriman Island
Letete Passage
Long Point
Long Eddy Point
Leonardville
Lower Neguac Wharf Range Back
Machais Seal Island
Mark Point
McColgan Point
Miscou Island
Mulholland Point
Musquash Head
Musquash Island
Oak Point
Partridge Island
Pea Point
Pointe du Chene Range
Point Escuminac
Point Lepreau
Pointe-Sapin Range Back Tower
Quaco Head
Richibucto Head

▾ **Cape Spear,** Newfoundland

◄ **Port au Choix,** Newfoundland

▲ **Battery Point Breakwater,** Nova Scotia

St. Modeste Island
Surgeon Cove Point
Tides Cove Point
Westport Cove
Woody Point

## NOVA SCOTIA

Abbot's Harbour
Annapolis
Apple River
Baccaro Point
Balache Point
Barrington
Bass River
Battery Point Breakwater
Bear River
Beaver Island

Belliveau's Cove (Le Phare de l'Anse)
Berry Head
Betty Island
Black Rock
Black Rock Point
Boar's Head
Bourgeois Inlet
Briar Island
Bunker Island
Burntcoat Head
Cameron Island
Candlebox Island
Canso Town (Canso Range)
Cape d'Or
Cape Forchu
Cape George (Antigonish)
Cape George (Richmond)
Cape Negro Island

▼ **Woody Point,** Newfoundland

▲ **Halifax Harbour,** Nova Scotia

Green Island (Richmond)
Gregory Island
Gull Rock (Lockeport)
Gunning Point Island
Guyon Island
Guysborough
Halifax Harbour
Hampton
Havre Boucher Range
Henry Island
Hog Island (Port Felix)
Horton Bluff
Ile Haute
Indian Harbour
Isaac's Harbour
Jeddore Rock
Jerome Point
Jerseyman Island
Kaulbach Island
Kidston Island
Liscomb Island
Little Hope Island
Little Narrows
Lockeport

Louisbourg
Low Point
Mabou
MacNeil Beach
Main-A-Dieu
Man Of War Point
Marache Point (Arichat)
Margaree Harbour
Margaree Island
Margaretville
Maugher Beach (Halifax Harbour)
Medway Head
Mitchener Point
Mosher Island
Mullin's Point
Musquodoboit Harbour
Neil Harbour
North Canso
Outer Island
Parrsboro
Pearl Island
Pease Island
Peggys Point
Pennant Point

▲ **Humber Bay,** Ontario

◀ **Fort Point,** Nova Scotia

Peter Island
Pictou Bar
Pictou Harbour
Pictou Island East
Pictou Island South
Pictou Island West
Point Aconi
Pomquet Island
Port Bickerton
Port George
Port Medway
Port Mouton
Prim Point
Pubnico Harbour
Pugwash (Fishing Point)
Quaker Island
Queensport
Rouse Point

Sable Island, East
Sable Island, West
Salvages (Half Moon)
Sambro Harbour
Sambro Island
Sandy Point
Scatarie
Schafner Point
Seal Island
Sheet Harbour
Sheet Rock
Spencer's Island
Spry Bay
St. Paul Island, Northeast
St. Paul Island, Southwest
Stoddard Island (Little St. Agnes)
Sydney Bar
Sydney Range

Terence Bay
Terminals Breakwater
Trenton East River
Tusket River
Victoria Beach
Wallace Harbour
Walton Harbour
Western Head
Westhaver Island
West Head
West Ironbound Island
White Head Island
Whitehead Island
Wood's Harbour

## ONTARIO

Badgeley Island
Blind River
Boyd Island
Brebeuf Island (Gin Rock)
Bruce Mines
Burlington Bay
The Bustards
Byng Inlet Range
Cabot Head
Cape Croker
Cape Robert
Christian Island
Clapperton Island
Collingwood
Coppermine Point
Cove Island
Flowerpot Island
French River Inner Range Lights
Gereaux Island
Giants Tomb
Gibraltar Point
Gore Bay
Great Duck Island
Griffith Island, Georgian Bay
Hope Island, Lake Erie
Humber Bay
Janet Head, North Channel
Jones Island, Parry Sound
Kagawong, Manitoulin Island
Killarney East, Georgian Bay
Killarney West

Kincardine
Lion's Head
Little Current
Lonely Island
Manitowaning
McKay Island
Meaford
Michael's Bay
Midland
Midland Point
Mississagi
Mississagi Strait
Narrow Island (Rabbit Island)
Nottawasaga
Old Thames River
Owen Sound
Penetanguishene
Point Abino, Lake Erie
Point Clark
Pointe au Baril
Port Burwell
Port Dalhousie
Presqu'ile
Providence Bay
Red Rock
Red Rock
Salmon Point (Wicked Point)
Snug Harbour
South Baymouth
Southhamption
Spruce Shoal
Strawberry Island
Sulphur Island
Thessalon
Thornbury
Thunder Bay
Tobermory
Turning Rock
Victoria Harbour
The Westerns
West Sister Rock
Windmill Point
Whiskey Island

▶▶ **Quaco Head,** New Brunswick

## PRINCE EDWARD ISLAND

Annandale Range Rear
Big Tignish (Jude's Point)
Blockhouse Point
Brighton Beach Range Front
Brighton Beach Range Rear
Brush Wharf Range Front
Cape Bear
Cape Egmont
Cape Tryon
Cascumpeque
Covehead Harbour (Cape Stanhope)
Douse Point Range Front
Douse Point Range Rear
East Point
Fish Island
Little Channel (Hardy's Channel) Range Rear
Georgetown Range Front
Georgetown Range Rear (St. Andrew's Point)

Haszard Point Range Front
Haszard Point Range Rear
Howard's Cove
Indian Head
Leards Range Front (Palmer Range Rear)
Leards Range Rear
Malpeque Harbour Approach Range Rear
Malpeque Outer (Darnley Point) Range Rear
Miminegash Range Rear
Murray Harbour Range Front (Murray Head)
Murray Harbour Range Rear
New London Range Rear (Yankee Hill)
North Cape
Northport Range Rear
North Rustico Harbour
Panmure Head
Prim Point (Point Prim)
Port Borden Pier
Port Borden Range Front
Port Borden Range Rear
Seacow Head

◀◀ **Port Dalhousie,** Ontario

▼ **Strawberry Island,** Ontario

◀ **Point Prim**, Prince Edward Island

▶▶ **Louisbourg**, Nova Scotia

Ile Verte
La Martre
Long Pilgrim
Natashquan Point
Petite Ile au Martinau
Petit-Métis
Pointe á la Renommée

Pointe au Pére
Pointe Carleton
Pointe des Monts
Pointe du Sud-Ouest
Pointe Noire
Rochers au Cormoran
St. Lawrence River
West Point

SASKATCHEWAN

Cochin

◄ **Avondale**, Nova Scotia

# RESOURCES

Bachand, Robert G. *Northeast Lights: Lighthouses and Lightships: Rhode Island to Cape May, New Jersey*. Norwalk, Connecticut: Sea Sports Publications, 1989.

Crompton, Samuel Willard and Michael J. Rhein. *The Ultimate Book of Lighthouses*. San Diego, California: Thunder Bay Press, 2003.

Jones, Ray. *The Lighthouse Encyclopedia: The Definitive Reference*. Guilford, Connecticut: The Globe Pequot Press, 2004.

Harrison, Tim and Ray Jones. *Lost Lighthouses*. Guilford, Connecticut: The Globe Pequot Press, 2000.

Marcus, John. *Lighthouses of New England*. Stillwater, Minnesota: Voyaguer Press, 2001.

Mitchell, Al. *Lighthouses of America*. Edison, New Jersey: Chartwell Books, 2007.

Noble, Dennis L. *Lighthouses and Keepers: The U.S. Lighthouse Service and Its Legacy*. Annapolis, Maryland: Naval Institute Press, 1997.

Roberts, Bruce and Ray Jones. *American Lighthouses: A Definitive Guide*. Guilford, Connecticut: The Globe Pequot Press, 2002.

The Lighthouse Directory. Rowlett, Russell J.
http://www.unc.edu/~rowlett/lighthouse/
(accessed June and July 2008)

Lighthousefriends.com. Anderson, Kraig
http://www.lighthousefriends.com (accessed June and July 2008)

National Park Service: U.S. Department of the Interior
http://www.nps.gov (accessed June and July 2008)

Mendocino Community Network
http://mcnsite.mcn.org/ (accessed June and July 2008)

American Lighthouse Foundation
http://www.lighthousefoundation.org/
(accessed June and July 2008)

U.S. Fish and Wildlife Service
http://www.fws.gov/ (accessed June and July 2008)

Lighthouse Getaway
http://www.lighthousegetaway.com/lights/
(accessed June and July 2008)

Rock Island Lighthouse Historical and Memorial Association
http://rockislandlighthouse.org/ (accessed June and July 2008)

Maritime Heritage Network
http://www.maritimeheritage.net/ (accessed June and July 2008)

Kennedy Space Center, NASA. U.S. Air Force: Latest Keepers of the Light. Mansfield, Cheryl L.
http://www.nasa.gov/centers/kennedy/about/history/lighthouse.html (accessed June and July 2008)

The Ponce de Leon Inlet Lighthouse Preservation Association
http://www.ponceinlet.org/ (accessed June and July 2008)

New England Lighthouses A Virtual Guide
http://www.lighthouse.cc/ (accessed June and July 2008)

The Lighthouse Depot Lighthouse Digest
http://www.lighthousedepot.com/ (accessed June and July 2008)

The Nova Scotia Lighthouse Preservation Society
http://www.nslps.com/ (accessed June and July 2008)

The Northern Lighthouse Board
http://www.nlb.org.uk/ (accessed June and July 2008)

The Horton Point Lighthouse. Muller, Robert G.
http://experts.longisland.com/lighthouses/archive_article.php?ExpArtID=1023 (accessed June and July 2008)

United States Lighthouse Society
http://www.uslhs.org/ (accessed June and July 2008)

The Commissioners of Irish Lights
http://www.cil.ie/ (accessed June and July 2008)

Seeing the Light Lighthouses of the Western Great Lakes
http://www.terrypepper.com/ (accessed June and July 2008)

▸▸**Brant Point**, Massachusetts

◀◀ **Pemaquid Point,** Maine

# ACKNOWLEDGMENTS & CREDITS

The author would like to acknowledge Jean Le Blanc, Juana Martinez, Ellie and Howie Yahm, Robert Arietta, and Kenneth Crossland for their support; Lucy and Fineas Jackson for their patience; and Aaron Murray, Brian MacMullen, and Sean Moore for the opportunity.

The publisher wishes to thank Kraig Anderson of Lighthouse Friends and Bryan Collars of the South Carolina Department of Archives and History.

Hylas Publishing
President: Sean Moore
Art Director: Brian MacMullen
Designers: Eunho Lee, Hwaim Holly Lee
Editors: Rachael Lanicci, Suzanne Lander, Casey Tolfree, Gabrielle Kappes, Susan Meigs, Lori Baird
Picture researcher: Ben DeWalt
Production editor: Eunoh Lee

The following abbreviations are used: NASA–National Aeronautics and Space Administration; NOAA–National Oceanic and Atmospheric Association; USCG–United States Coast Guard; BSP–BigStockPhoto; ISP–iStockphoto; SS–Shutterstock; IO–IndexOpen; LOC–Library of Congress; JI–© 2008 Jupiterimages Corporation; WI–Wikimedia; SI–Smithsonian Institution; BLM–Bureau of Land Management
(t=top; b=bottom; l=left; r=right; c=center)

### Cover
Front/Back SS/Stephen B. Goodwin; Back SS/John Wollwerth

### Introduction
3 Sashidhar Nivarthi 4 IO/Mark Windom 6 SS/William J. Mahnken 8 LOC 1t SS/Magdalena Bujak 1b JI 2 SS/Anita Colic 3 BSP/Martin Mullen 4 WI/Alessio Damato 5bl LOC 5tr LOC 6-7 LOC 7 LOC 8 LOC 9 USCG

### Conical & Cylindrical Construction
18-19 ISP/Jeffrey Crider 20 SS/Aaron Kohr 21 SS/Lloyd S Clements 22 ISP/Dave Logan 23 BSP/Sally Scott 24 ISP/Jason Maehl 25 BSP/Mike Brake 26tl BSP/Melissa Riopel 26bl BSP/Scott Frangos 26-27 BML 27 ISP/Sherri Camp 28 BSP/Sherri Camp 28-29 BSP/Ron Bomund 29 BSP/Kenneth Keith Stilger 30 SS/Michael Rickard 31 JI 32 SS/Michael Rickard 33 SS/Ronald Sherwood 34 SS/David Gaylor 35 SS/FloridaStock 36tl NOAA/Collection of Elinor Dewire, Sentinel Publications 44bl SS/David Gaylor 45 IO/Mark Windom 46 Elinor DeWire, Sentinel Publications 39 NASA 40 NASA 41tl NASA 41tc NASA 41tr NASA 41br NASA 42 ISP/Jeffrey Crider 43 ISP/Kristin Kanan 44 Library of Congress 44-45 Library of Congress 45 Library of Congress 46-47 SS/FloridaStock 46 BSP/David Barth 47 BSP/James Steidl 48 SS/Mary Terriberry 57 SS/John Fuller 58 SS/Jill Lang 59 SS/Jeffrey Stone 60 SS/Ryan Arnaudin 53t SS/Jeffrey Stone 53b SS/catnap 54 SS/Gina Smith 55 SS/Gina Smith 56 BSP/Penny Williams 57 SS/Keith Murphy 58tl BSP/Mike Clendenen 58-59 BSP/Robert Byron 59 BSP/Robert Byron 60 ISP/Kenneth C. Zirkel 61 ISP/Eric Dunetz 62 SXU/Andy Ellingwood 63 SS/Andrea LG Ferguson 64 SS/Mark R 65 SS/Harris Shiffman 66 BSP/Paula Stephens 67 BSP 68 SS/Teresa Levite 69 LOC 70 LOC 71 LOC 74 Tim Pierce 74 LOC 80t LOC 80b LOC 81 LOC 83 SS/Paula Stephens 84 ISP/William Britten 77 NOAA/Mr. Steve Nicklas 78-79 SS/Greg Kushmerek 80 WI/JeremyA 81 BSP/Robert Goode 82 ISP/William Britten 83 LOC 84l LOC 84r LOC 85 LOC 86 BSP/Marilyn Wheeler 87 BSP/Paula Stephens 88 ISP/Jan Tyler 89 ISP/Charlotte Railton 90t BSP/Bradley Bellas 90b Archival Photograph by Steve Nicklas 91 SS/Erik Patton 92 SS/Michael Rickard 93tl WI 93br LOC 94 LOC 95 LOC 96 ISP/Loren Rodgers 97 ISP/Larry Workman 98 ISP/William Britten 99 ISP/Sterling Stevens 100 ISP/Arthur Preston 101t ISP/Micheal Chambers 102 BSP/Aaron Whitney 103 BSP/Aaron Whitney 104 ISP/Dave Logan 105 LOC 106 SS/David Gaylor 107t NOAA/Elinor DeWire, Sentinel Publications 107b WI/Jon Zander 108 SS/Mary Terriberry 109 SS/Gary W. Parker 110 SS/Bartosz Wardzinski 111 SS/Michelle Marsan 112 BSP/Jack Kunnen 113 SS/Roonie_70 114 BSP/Ann Horn 114-115 ISP/Dean Pennala 116 Sashidhar Nivarthi 117 Sashidhar Nivarthi 118 Sashidhar Nivarthi 119t Sashidhar Nivarthi 119b Sashidhar Nivarthi 120t BSP/Sam Aronov 120b BSP/Ken Griffith 121 BSP/Sam Aronov 122 SS/Bartosz Wardzinski 123 SS/Cynthia Kidwell 124 JI 125 Wi/Jauerback 126 ISP/Trevor Hunt 127 BSP/Amy N. Harris 128 ISP/Tum Tunthatakas 129 ISP/Joel Messner 130 ISP/Eugene Llacuna 131 ISP/Jim Mangione 132 ISP/Stephen Bonk 133 SS/Michael Hynes 134 ISP/Kathy Hicks 135 ISP/Kathy Hicks 136 SS/E. Sweet 137 SS/E. Sweet 138 SS/E. Sweet 139 SS/E. Sweet 140tr SS/Sean Nel 132b SS/Tom Hirtreiter 133tl SS/Lowe Llaguno 142 LOC 143t LOC 143br LOC 144tl LOC 144b LOC 145tl LOC 145b LOC

### Square Construction
146-147 SS/Zach Frank 148 BSP/Jenny Solomon 149 BSP/Shawn McGill 150 ISP/Stefano Dominici 151 SS/V. J. Matthew 152 BSP/Cindy Haggerty 153 SS/Alex Neauville 154 SS/Alex Neauville 155 SS/Alex Neauville 156 BSP/Chris Martin 157 SS/Mary Terriberry 158 BSP/Cathy Kovarik 159 BSP/Cathy Kovarik 160 ISP/Mark Coffey 161 BSP/Maria Dryfhout 162 BSP/Maria Dryfhout 163t ISP/Mark Coffey 163b BSP/Maria Dryfhout 163 BSP/Lijuan Guo 165 BSP/Jonathan Timar 166 SS/Sherri R. Camp 167tl SI 159bl LOC 168tr WI/Tim Herrick 168bl WI/Hannes Grobe 168tr WI/Adolphe Ganot 168br SS/Diane N. Ennis 169l SS/FloridaStock 169r WI

### Ocatgonal & Hexagonal Construction
170-171 BSP/Sreedhar Yedlapati 172 SS/Mary Terriberry 173 SS/Jason Tench 174 SS/Harris Shiffman 175l SS/Mary Terriberry 175r SS/Harris Shiffman 176 ISP/Joe Klune 177 SS/Diane N. Ennis 178 ISP/Joe Klune 179t BSP/Steven Hebert 179b ISP/Joe Klune 180 ISP/Michael Zak 181 LOC 174 ISP/Darius Sutherland 183t NOAA/Archival Photo by Mr. Steve Nicklas 183b JI 176 ISP/Chen Chun Wu 185 BSP/George Maina 186 ISP/Chiya Li 187t ISP/Chiya Li 187b SS/Kevin R Williams 188 LOC 181 ISP/Yungshu Chao 190 Shutterstock 191 ISP/Dominik Dabrowski 192t SXC/Sue R B 192-193 ISP/Jeffrey Crider 193t IO/Keith Levit Photography 194t SS/Matthew Jacques 194b SS/Norman Pogson 195 SS/Eriendur Konradsson 196 BSP/Andrew Kazmierski 197 BSP/Andrew Kazmierski 198t ISP/Andrew F Kazmierski 198b SS/Michael Hynes 199 BSP/James Van Wagenen 200 SS/David Gaylor 201 ISP/Wayne Howard 202 BSP/Steve Dunn 203 SS/Aron Brand 204 BSP/David Dorner 205t WI/United States Navy, Photographer's Mate 1st Class Ken Riley 213b BSP/G. Bryan Miller 214 SS/Ronald Sherwood 215 SS/LaNae Christenson 208 IO/Ron Chapple 209 IO 210 IO/Ron Chapple 211 IO/Ron Chapple 212 IO/Ron Chapple 213l IO 213r SS/David Kay 214 SS/Xuanlu Wang 215 ISP/Luis Camargo 216 BSP/Stephen Strathdee 217 ISP/Sean Wood 218 SS/David Gaylor 219 ISP/blphotocorp/Luis Camargo 220 BSP/Stephen Strathdee 221 BSP/Sean Wood 222 BSP/Michael Dalton 223 ISP/Curt Pickens 224 ISP/WMI Photography/Americus Times-Recorder 225 SS/David Davis 226 ISP/William Dellinger 227 ISP/William Dellinger 228 ISP/Margaret Marvin 229 BSP/George Maina 230 SS/Hiep Nguyen 231 BSP/Lee Reitz 232 BSP/Natalia Bratslavsky 233t BSP/Lee Reitz 233b IO/Mark Windom 234 SS/Lowe Llaguno 235tl LOC 235br USCG 236 ISP/Rockcoast sports/RCS GRAPHIX 237t BSP/Peter Anderson 237b ISP/Kacey Baxter 238t SS/Bill Kennedy 238b ISP/Kenneth C. Zirkel 239 BSP/Steve Dunn

### Skeletal Construction
240-241 BSP/Paul Brennan 242 BSP/Nathaniel Luckhurst 243 BSP/Ann Horn 244 BSP/David Crippen 245 BSP/Ann Horn 2468 BSP/Larry Jordan 247 BSP/Larry Jordan 248 John Keyes/www.johnkeyes.com 249 ISP/Ron Bergeron 250 Kraig Anderson/www.lighthousefriends.com 251 South Carolina Department of Archives and History 252 Purdue9394 253 Joseph White 254t Chad McDermott 254b JolaM 255 Coast to Coast Photography 256 Mitch Aunger 257t Mitch Aunger 257b Mitch Aunger 258 SS/Sebastien Windal 260t ISP/Lara Seregni 260b SS/E.G.Pors 261l SS/KML 261r BSP/Joanna Pickelsimer 262 IO/LLC, Vstock 263t BSP/Mario Savoia 263b LOC 264 LOC 265t ISP/John Pischke 265b LOC 266 ISP/Jennifer Trenchard 267 IO/LLC, Vstock

### List of North American Lights
268-269 SS/Andy Z. 270 SS/Yare Marketing 271 SS/Gordon Logue 272 SS/Aaron Bunker 273 SS/Jill Battaglia 274 WI/Lorax 275 SS/Rebecca Photography 276 SS/Rick S 277 SS/Chee-Onn Leong 279 SS/Jim Parkin 280 SS/Jim Parkin 281 SS/David A Yohnka 282 SS/Paula Stephens 283 SS/Dee Golden 284 WI/Cacophony 285 WI/EncMstr 286-287 SS/Mary Terriberry 288 ISP/Todd Smith 289 SS/David Watkins 291 ISP/Larry Masseth 292 SS/Hugo de Wolf 295 SS/Phil Berry 296 SS/Jason Kasumovic 297 SS/C. Rene Ammundsen 298 SS/Vlad Ghiea 299 SS/Richard Fitzer 300 SXC/Dave Dyet 301 SS/Allan Morrison 302 SS/Mark Plummer 303 SS/David Gaylor 304 ISP/Denis Tangney 305 IO/Getty Images - Photo Disc 306 ISP/Brian Swartz 307 SS/Sergei A. Tkachenko 309 ISP/Jason Verschoor 310 iStockphoto 311 ISP/Neil Kinnear 312 ISP/Denise Tayntor 313 SS/Shane Thomas Shaw 314 ISP/Oliver Childs 316 SS/mirounga 318 SS/spirit of america